The Austrian Solution

International Conflict
and Cooperation

THE
AUSTRIAN
SOLUTION

International
Conflict and
Cooperation

Edited by

Robert A. Bauer

Published for the Johns Hopkins
Foreign Policy Institute, School of
Advanced International Studies
The Johns Hopkins University by
the University Press of Virginia
Charlottesville

THE UNIVERSITY PRESS OF VIRGINIA

Copyright © 1982 by the Rector and Visitors
of the University of Virginia

First published 1982

Martin F. Herz, "Allied Occupation of Austria:
The Early Years," © 1982 by Martin F. Herz.

The editor and publisher are grateful to
Siegler & Co. for permission to reprint the
following: William L. Stearman, "An Analysis
of Soviet Objectives in Austria," from *The
Soviet Union and the Occupation of Austria*,
by William L. Stearman, © 1962 by William L.
Stearman.

Hanspeter Neuhold, "Permanent Neutrality and
Nonalignment: Similarities and Differences,"
first appeared in India Quarterly, July-
September 1979; reprinted by permission of the
Indian Council of World Affairs, New Delhi.

Library of Congress Cataloging in Publication
Data
Main entry under title:

The Austrian solution—international conflict
   and cooperation.

   Includes bibliographical references.
   1. Austria--Foreign relations--1945-   --Ad-
dresses, essays, lectures. I. Bauer, Robert A.
DB99.2.A83   327.436   81-21916
ISBN 0-8139-0903-1   AACR2

Printed in the United States of America

CONTENTS

Foreword
Twenty-five years after
the Austrian State Treaty

In terms of history, a quarter of a century is hardly more than a fraction of a second. Yet, the twenty-five years since the signing of the Austrian State Treaty on May 15, 1955, have given us sufficient time and distance to evaluate this event that we Austrians consider a cornerstone of post-World War II history. Has Austria, by pursuing a policy of active neutrality, contributed to easing east-west tensions and to the preservation of world peace? We Austrians like to think we have.

My associates and I have pondered these and other questions when discussing plans to commemorate the State Treaty anniversary in the United States. We expected relatively little interest from the United States concerning how a small nation thousands of miles away has fared since it regained its freedom and independence, considering the country's preoccupation with the fierce 1980 presidential election campaign under way, the hostage crisis still unsolved, and economic problems confronting it.

To our surprise and delight, the reaction of our American friends to our suggestion that they join us in taking stock of Austria's most recent history was enthusiastic. Many highly distinguished historians, diplomats, former members of the U.S. armed forces, and journalists made themselves available to compare notes with our historians in four symposia on the Austrian State Treaty, of which three took place in Washington, D.C., and one in New York City.

I am very pleased and greatly honored to have been asked to introduce this publication of some

of the presentations and discussions from the
symposia at American University, Washington,
D.C., and Columbia University, jointly presented
by the Institute of War and Peace Studies, the
School of International Affairs, and the Austrian Institute, New York. This publication
will certainly be considered one of the most
valuable contributions to Austria's postwar history by students and scholars interested in our
country.

I will not detain you for long from the most
interesting papers presented by this group of
highly qualified experts, some of whom I can
describe as witnesses to history, since they
have been in some influential positions in the
U.S. High Commissions for Austria and the U.S.
Armed Forces in Austria whereby they were involved in the treaty-negotiating process.

Among the many aspects of the treaty's history the contributors analyzed the different
policies and motives pursued by the four occupying powers—Great Britain, France, the United
States, and the Soviet Union—vis-à-vis Austria.
You will read of many frustrating periods of
deadlock during the treaty negotiations, when
Austria became a pawn in the cold war between
East and West. I believe, however, that the
key factor in the final execution of the treaty was the staunch determination of the Austrian people and of their leaders to achieve
freedom and independence. This devotion to
freedom within a democratic state is as strong
today as it was during the ten trying years of
four-power military occupation.

The authors also deal with a suggestion that
they try to use Austrian neutrality as a model
for a political solution of the crisis over
Afghanistan. I agree with the conclusions of
these experts that Austria's neutrality is not
readily transposable to Afghanistan. The basic

element of Austria's neutrality is the fact
that it was chosen by the free will of the
Austrian people and was a give-and-take solution within the East-West context with every-
body gaining in the long run. I realize that
when a neutral Austria was first proposed by
our government, the idea met with little enthusiasm from Washington and was answered by
Moscow with a clear *nyet*. At that time, our
American friends considered neutrality to be
something ominous, a cop-out from defending
democratic ideals.

I believe that twenty-five years of Austria's
policy of active neutrality have proven these
fears to be totally unfounded. Austria, a
genuine member of the camp of democratic nations, is speaking out openly about what it
believes in at home as well as within the community of the United Nations. Austria's view
of neutrality is certainly not "ideological
neutralism." Austria will, as it has pledged,
endeavor with all means at its disposal to pro-
mote peace and understanding among nations, offering—when asked by the parties involved—its
services as a mediator. As it has in the past,
Austria will continue to open its borders to
peoples persecuted because of their race, religion, or political convictions.

Let me conclude by expressing my sincere
gratitude to all the participants in the Austrian Treaty symposia in Washington, D.C. and
New York City and to those who helped in organizing them. I wish to thank Professor Dr.
Robert Bauer particularly for arranging the
symposium at American University and for making
this publication possible.

Dr. Karl Herbert Schober
Austrian Ambassador to the United States
Washington, D.C., 1977-81

Preface

The two symposia* leading to the publication of these essays were designed to bring to bear a broad spectrum of expertise on this important chapter of contemporary history. We were fortunate to be able to assemble American and Austrian scholars and diplomats as well as an impressive number of American participants in the political, military, and economic decision-making areas during the period 1945-55. The biographical sketches of the contributors at the back of the book underline their connection with the period under discussion.

My introductory overview of the First Austrian Republic from 1918 to 1938 is designed to familiarize the reader, particularly American students of Austrian affairs, with the political, economic, cultural, and ideological problems of Austrian society during this period. It sets the stage for a comparison with the fundamentally different developments in the second Austrian republic after World War II. The contributors then analyzed step by step the internal developments in Austria between 1945 and

---

*The Austrian Solution—The History of a West-East Accord, at American University in Washington, D.C., on April 8, 1980. Towards the Austrian State Treaty: America's Austrian Policies 1945-55 on October 17, 1980 at Columbia University, jointly sponsored with the Austrian Institute, New York City.

1955, the policy formulations and decisions of
the occupying powers, and the concept of Austrian neutrality.

Martin F. Herz deals with the effects of Soviet
behavior in Austria and with the four-power re-
lationships. Halvor O. Ekern describes the
operations of the Allied Commission for Austria
and the importance of the strikes of 1950, an
occurrence elaborated upon by Adolf Sturmthal.
The latter also records the decisive contribution of the Austrian Labor Unions to internal
stability and resistance to Communist subversion.

Ware Adams, the author of both the essay on
and the concept of the "negative veto," analyzes
the process that was involved in reaching this
important turning point in the four-power occupation policies.

William B. Bader renders an account of the
formulation and execution of U.S. policy towards
Austria and William L. Stearman attempts to dis-
cern Soviet political, military and economic
considerations in the treaty making. Manfried
Rauchensteiner presents his views on the treaty
and its consequences.

The application of the Austrian model to
present-day crisis situations, like Afghanistan,
is considered by Robert G. Neumann. Neutrality,
as conceived and practiced by the Austrians, is
described by Fritz Bock, and Hanspeter Neuhold
discusses the important distinction between
neutrality and nonalignment; although these two
contributors could not attend the symposia, we
were nonetheless fortunate to have their essays
in this volume.

Concluding remarks and observations from the
Columbia University conference by the late
Charles W. Yost summarize, in effect, the consensus reached on the reasons for the successful conclusion of the State Treaty: effective
crisis management, political and military

restraint, the pursuit of professional diplomacy, constructive economic policies, and Austrian statesmanship of the highest order.

We gratefully acknowledge our indebtedness to Consul Dr. Fritz Cocron, Director of the Austrian Institute in New York City, for organizing the Columbia University conference and for his assistance in the publication of this volume. We are also obligated to Mr. Richard L. Apperson, Associate Dean, School of Public and International Affairs, American University, Washington, D.C., for his substantial contribution to the success of the April symposium.

Robert A. Bauer

Washington, D.C., 1981

Introduction

As a young assistant to Secretary of State Dean G. Acheson, I attended a Foreign Ministers' Meeting in Paris in 1945. I vividly recall Ambassador Charles E. Bohlen emerging from one of the sessions and telling me with a broad smile: "I think we have it." He referred to the possible conclusion of a state treaty with Austria. Though declared to be a victim of Nazi aggression that should be treated as a liberated country after the war, Austria at that time was still under four-power occupation and under supervision of the Allied Council, consisting of the United States, France, Great Britain, and the Soviet Union. Ambassador Bohlen's optimistic view of the progress of the negotiations was not borne out by events. It took another six years of hard bargaining, quiet diplomacy, and astute policies by the Austrian government leaders to achieve the long-desired result.

The treaty was signed in May 1955. It ended the occupation of the country and restored its independence. As part of the settlement, the Austrian Parliament passed a constitutional amendment declaring Austria's neutrality in perpetuity. The treaty, at least so far, takes a unique place in post-World War II history. It led to the withdrawal of Soviet forces from a country in the center of Europe, made possible the development of a prosperous Austria, and established Vienna as the third United Nations city after New York and Geneva. At the time of this writing, an Austrian serves his second term as secretary-general of the United Nations.

Austria has followed an independent and largely pro-Western foreign policy, while strictly
observing her commitment to neutrality. The
political and military balance of Europe was
clearly influenced, with some advantage to the
West and some to the East.

The twenty-fifth anniversary of the signing
of the treaty was commemorated in 1980 in Vienna
and other world capitals. In a period of high
international tensions, it provided diplomats
and scholars of many nations with the opportunity to review the history of the treaty making
and to reflect on possible lessons to be learned
for the solution of contemporary international
conflicts. In the United States, major symposia
dealing with the treaty were held in Washington,
D.C., and New York City. They brought together
American and Austrian experts who considered,
debated, and supplemented basic papers on the
topic. The symposium at American University in
Washington, D.C., was organized by Dr. Robert A.
Bauer, who was also one of the two moderators
at the symposium at Columbia University sponsored by the Austrian Consulate General and the
Austrian Cultural Institute. Dr. Bauer, a re-
tired senior U.S. foreign service officer and
the editor of two volumes on American foreign
policy and international economic policies, has
put together a collection of essays and summaries from the Washington and New York symposia.
They serve to establish a historical record and
to analyze the motivations of the participating
powers and the changes in the military balance
of power, as well as to judge the pertinence of
the negotiating process and conclusion of the
treaty to present-day West-East problems.

The strong interest in the "Austrian solution" was evidenced by the great success of a
session held at the Johns Hopkins Foreign Policy Institute in October 1980, at which Austrian

experts Professor Gerald Stourzh and Dr. Manfried Rauchensteiner presented excellent essays—
followed by a lively discussion with faculty
members and graduate students.

I believe that the academic and foreign-policy
utility of this volume is very high indeed. It
will contribute to a fuller understanding of the
historical events in the period from 1945 to
1955, of the intricacies of foreign-policy decision making, and of the negotiating process involved in the settlement of West-East problems
and conflicts.

Lucius D. Battle, Chairman
Johns Hopkins Foreign Policy Institute

Washington, D.C., 1981

The Austrian Solution

International Conflict
and Cooperation

ROBERT A. BAUER

Austria 1918–38
An Overview

Austria's road from the First Republic to the
Second Republic was marked by tragedies, suffer-
ings, violence, inner dissension, and political
ineptitude. Outside Austria, this was comple-
mented by the inconsistent and contradictory
policies of the major powers. If we wish to understand the setting for the events from 1945 to
1955, a brief review of the political, economic,
cultural, and ideological underpinnings of the
period is advisable.

*The whole modern history of German-Austria is
colored by the opposition between German and
Austrian sympathies. The Austro-German middle
class came into existence during the century between 1750 and 1850. The young intellectuals
who were reared in the hatred of the absolutism
of Metternich and who absorbed the ideas of
aspiring European liberalism, fell under the
German influences of their time. Ever since
that time, German and Austrian influences have
struggled for mastery in the soul of Austria.*

Those are the words of Dr. Otto Bauer, foremost
theoretician and politician of the Austrian
Social Democratic Party, in his book *The Austrian Revolution* (p. 25).
    Professor Carl E. Schorske, in his volume *Fin-
de-Siècle Vienna: Politics and Culture,* sees
that Austrian liberalism ended in 1848. Later,

its social base remained weak, confined to the middle-class Germans and German Jews of the urban centers. New social groups—the peasantry, the urban artisans and workers, and the Slavic peoples—laid claims to political participation. In the 1880s these groups formed mass parties to challenge the liberal hegemony: namely, the anti-Semitic Christian Socials and Pan-Germans and the Social Democrats and Slavic nationalists.

At the end of the last century, two men began to exercise great political influence on the Christian Social and Pan-German groups. They were the charismatic mayor of Vienna, Karl Lueger, and Georg von Schönerer. In American terms, both could be called populists. Both elevated anti-Semitism to a basic article of faith. But there was a clear-cut difference between their anti-Semitic approaches. When Lueger was ridiculed by the Socialist opposition in the Vienna City Council for being anti-Semitic although he played cards with Jewish friends in the coffeehouse, he responded with the phrase: "Who is a Jew is something I determine" (quoted in Schorske, p. 145); on the other hand, Schönerer attacked the Jews as "the sucking vampire" (Schorske, p. 128), and emphasized the racist approach by declaring: "Religion is of no importance, the nastiness lies in the race."

As the conflict of the Slavic nationalities with the German-speaking Austrians and the Hungarians became more acute, German nationalistic tendencies and sympathies became stronger among the German Austrians. When the Austro-Hungarian Empire came to an end in November 1918, it was logical and inevitable, in terms of the nationalistic, cultural, and economic considerations of that traumatic year in Austria's history, that the provisional republican parliament .

declared that German-Austria (Deutschösterreich) was a part of the new German Republic.

The decision to join the German Republic was
also based on the belief in the implementation
of U.S. President Woodrow Wilson's Point Ten of
his Fourteen Points, which read: "The peoples
of Austria-Hungary, whose place among the nations we wish to see safeguarded and assured,
should be accorded the freest opportunity of
autonomous development" (Lansing, *The Peace
Negotiations*, p. 315). That such a move was envisioned by the U.S. government can be seen in
the semiofficial interpretation of the Fourteen
Points, prepared under the supervision of Col.
Edward House by Frank Cobb and Walter Lippmann.
Under Point Nine it says: "In the region of
Trent the Italians claim a strategic rather than
ethnic frontier. It should be noted in this
connection that Italy and Germany will become
neighbours if German-Austria joins the *German
Empire*" (*Foreign Relations of the United States*,
1918, p. 407) (emphasis supplied). That the
continuance of a German empire joined by the
German-speaking part of the Austro-Hungarian
Empire was contemplated by the U.S. government
just a few weeks before the end of the war can
be seen in a memorandum drawn up by the American Secretary of State Robert Lansing, dated
September 21, 1918, and published in 1920. It
proposed the dissolution of the Habsburg Monarchy; the establishment of independent national
states of Czechs, Serbs, Croats, Slovenes, and
Poles; and for the remainder of Austria: "Reduction of Austria to the ancient boundaries
and title the Archduchy of Austria. Incorporation of Archduchy in the Imperial German Confederation" (Lansing, *The Peace Negotiations*,
pp. 192, 195).

In fact, there is documentary evidence that
there had been great hopes on the Allied side

that Austria-Hungary could be dealt with separately, particularly in view of the peace overtures of Emperor Charles, who through his brother-in-law, Prince Sixtus, had expressed his willingness for a separate peace. This secret move was revealed by French Prime Minister Clemenceau on April 12, 1917, when he publicized the Austrian emperor's letter of March 17, and Secretary of State Robert Lansing called Clemenceau's action "a piece of the most astounding stupidity for which no sufficient excuse can be made" and added "His disclosure has thrown Austria bodily into the arms of Germany" (Lansing, *War Memoirs*, pp. 264 ff.). Some circles in the Allied countries had an uneasy feeling that the breaking up of the buffer between Pan-Germanism and Pan-Slavism might have grave consequences for the future power constellation in Europe. In his book *The Gathering Storm*, Winston Churchill called the complete breakup of the Austro-Hungarian Empire by the treaties of St.-Germain and Trianon a cardinal tragedy. He wrote:

For centuries this surviving embodiment of the Holy Roman Empire had afforded a common life, with advantages in trade and security, to a large number of peoples, none of whom in our time had the strength or vitality to stand by themselves in the face of pressure from a revivified Germany or Russia. All these races wished to break away from the federal or imperial structure, and to encourage their desires was deemed a liberal policy. The Balkanisation of Southeastern Europe proceeded apace, with the consequent relative aggrandisement of Prussia and the German Reich, which, though tired and war-scarred, was intact and locally overwhelming. There is not one of the peoples or provinces that constituted the Empire of the Habsburgs to whom gaining

their independence has not brought the tortures
which ancient poets and theologians had reserved
for the damned. The noble capital of Vienna,
the home of so much long-defended culture and
tradition, the centre of so many roads, rivers,
and railways, was left stark and starving, like
a great emporium in an impoverished district
whose inhabitants have mostly departed (p. 10).

Before becoming the last Habsburg emperor,
Archduke Charles told his spouse, Archduchess
Zita, in August of 1914 that after the war there
"will be two purely German Empires in the heart
of Europe with a big Slav group alongside them.
Or, more likely, the Slav group will be pulled
to Russia and we in turn will be swallowed up
by Prussia" (Shepherd, p. 153).

On November 11, 1918, a few minutes after the
noon hour, Charles I signed the manifesto in
which he renounced all participation in the affairs of state and declared: "I recognize in
advance whatever decision that German-Austria
may make about its future political form. The
people, through its representatives, has taken
over the government. May the people of German-
Austria, in unity and tolerance, create and
strengthen the new order! Only an inner peace
can heal the wounds of this war."

This inner peace was to be long in coming!
On November 12 the Republic of German-Austria
(Republik Deutschösterreich) was formally proclaimed by the provisional national assembly in
Vienna. The Social Democrats voted unanimously
for the republic and so did most of the Christian Socials—with the exception of three, including later-President Wilhelm Miklas, who
voted against the word *republic* in the new
basic state law. Article I of the state law
proclaimed Austria a "democratic Republic" and
Article II declared "German-Austria is a constituent part of the German Republic."

The Treaty of Saint-Germain, signed on September 10, 1919, put an end to the *Anschluss* idea. But it was firmly rooted in the goals of the political left and in those of the Pan-Germans on the right. The deep economic troubles besetting the new republic were another factor underlying the desire to join a greater national and economic body.

Dr. Otto Bauer wrote in his book *The Austrian Revolution:* "The idea that an epoch of social revolution would involve the break up of Austria into free national States and the union of German-Austria with the rest of Germany had been part of the political tradition of Social Democracy in Austria since its inception" (p. 26). And in the same book, he wrote:

With the collapse of its rule over the other nations, German-Austria's historical mission was ended, for the sake of which she had hitherto willingly borne the separation from the German Motherland. The Germans in Bohemia, Silesia, Northern Moravia, and the German Alpine lands, separated by Czech territory, had no other choice than between Czech alien rule and union with Germany. How helpless Austria was on her own legs when faced with the new national States, was discovered in the first stages of the revolution. Austria was overtaken by hunger. Immediately, the Czechs suspended the export of foodstuffs and coal. The first step which the nascent Austrian State was obliged to take was to request the Berlin Government to furnish assistance in the form of cereals. Standing alone Austria could not possibly maintain her economic position in face of the hostility of the new national States. The economic losses caused by these national and territorial defections could only be compensated by the support of the economically stronger Empire. During October 1918

*large sections of the middle classes, especially
the intellectual classes, began to hope that
union with Germany would offer some compensation
for the collapse of their edifice of domination*
(pp. 61 ff.).

As foreign secretary of the republican government, Otto Bauer reached an agreement with the
German Foreign Minister, Count Brockdorff-
Rantzau, on the conditions for the incorporation of Austria into the German Reich.

In summary, it can be said that at the birth
of the First Austrian Republic there were nationalistic, political, ideological, and economic motivations for joining the newly established German Republic. And, there remained
until the Dollfuss-Schuschnigg era an undercur-
rent of Anschluss feeling throughout the country.

Blockaded by all the neighboring states and
suffering acutely from a shortage of commodities
and the refusal of foreign countries to accept
Austrian currency—the crown—Austria was bound
to experience a considerable fall in the value
of that currency. Once the harsh peace conditions became known, confidence in Austria's
economic future was shattered. Foreign specu-
lators unloaded their stocks of crowns, and Austrians sold their crown-securities in order to
buy foreign bills and securities. The currency
depreciation pauperized large sections of the
citizenry. During the war a good part of the
liquid capital had been converted into war-loan
certificates. The republic paid the interest
on the war loans, but in paper crowns. As the
value of the crown sank, the rentiers were
literally expropriated. In 1922, the state
paid the rentiers a ten-thousandth part of the
crown's nominal value.

As Dr. Otto Bauer was the most influential
leader on the left, so Dr. Ignaz Seipel, a Roman

Catholic priest and the leader of the Christian
Socials, was the recognized leader of the conservatives. The republic had essentially a two-
party system, Social Democrat and Christian Social. Two small parties, the Pan-Germans and
the *Landbund* (an agrarian interest party), each
occupied a handful of seats in the 165-member
Nationalrat (the Lower House). The Communists
captured only four seats in the first election
and were then never able to muster enough votes
for even one seat until the establishment of
the Second Austrian Republic—when they again
captured only a few seats in the first elections. The coalition government, Christian Social and Social Democrat, lasted until October
1920, and from then on the Christian Socials,
supported by the agricultural *Landbund* organized the government until the republic ceased
to exist in April 1934 and was replaced on May 1
of that year by the corporate Federal State of
Austria (Bundesstaat Österreich).

As the economic crisis approached total collapse of the system, Chancellor Seipel departed
on August 20, 1922, for Prague, Berlin, and
Verona. When he reached Verona, it became known
that he had offered Italy a currency and customs
union with Austria. Italy and Austria were to
form one unit for currency purposes, and thus
Austria would avoid the final currency catas-
trophe. Austria was to accept an Italian political and economic protectorate. Considering the
great unpopularity of Italy in Austria at that
time, Seipel's move was interpreted by many observers as a shrewd maneuver—drawing the world's
attention to Austria's plight and based on the
calculation that both Yugoslavia and Czechoslovakia would oppose the union. And so it was.
The Entente powers and Czechoslovakia worked out
a deal. Under a loan guarantee, the Austrian

currency converted into the schilling at 14,000
old crowns for one schilling. Indirectly, the
agreement reconfirmed the ban on an Anschluss.
A League of Nations general commissioner and a
committee composed of the representatives of the
powers that had guaranteed the Austrian loan
exercised a vast control over Austrian economic
policies. The republic's sovereignty was clearly limited. The League of Nations' financial
control ended on June 30, 1926.

The domestic political scene during the period
1918-38 was characterized by an increasing po-
larization of the population and the confrontation between the "Blacks" (Christian Socials)
and the "Reds" (Social Democrats). In addition
to existing army, gendarmerie, and police, the
opponents organized private militias: the Social
Democrats, the Republican *Schutzbund* ("Republican protection organization"), and an independent conservative militia, the *Heimwehr* ("home
guard").

Under the intellectual leadership of Otto
Bauer the Social Democrats espoused and adhered
to classical Marxist principles, reaffirmed in
their party platform adopted in Linz on November
3, 1926. Simply looking over the contents of
Bauer's volume, *The Austrian Revolution*, one can
ascertain the party's basic ideology:

Part III—The Predominance of the Working Class.
        The State and the Working Class.

Part IV—The Period of the Balance of Class
        Power.
        Revolutionary and Counterrevolutionary
        Forces.
        The Struggle against the Counter-
        revolution.

Part   V—The Restoration of the Bourgeoisie.

The following dates mark the milestones on the road to final disaster:

March 11, 1926: First march of the *Heimwehr* in a strongly Socialist district of Vienna.

July 15-17, 1927: After the acquittal of three defendants on trial for killing two people when they fired on leftists, bloody riots occurred in Vienna. Fire was set to the Palace of Justice. (In the same year, the unemployment rate reached 21.7 percent.)

October 8, 1928: Parallel demonstrations of the *Heimwehr* and the *Schutzbund* in Wiener Neustadt, separated by a cordon of the regular army.

September 16, 1929: Collapse of the Creditanstalt-Bankverein, setting in motion the great economic world crisis.

October 27, 1929: *Heimwehr* demonstration in Vienna.

May 18, 1930: The "Korneuburg Oath" of the *Heimwehr*, reaffirming determination for conservative action.

November 9, 1930: Last parliamentary elections before the second World War.

May 12, 1931: Governmental action to save the Creditanstalt. (In the same year, an attempt by Austria and Germany to form a customs union was vetoed by France.)

September 12-13, 1931: Attempted coup d'état by the Styrian Home guard, "The Pfriemer Putsch."

On May 20, 1932, Dr. Engelbert Dollfuss, a Christian Social politician, was named chancellor. On March 4, 1933, following a violent debate in the parliament, the three presidents of

the lower house resigned from their offices.
Based on a constitutional technicality—that the
parliament had to be convened by one of its
presidents—the Dollfuss government blocked further parliamentary sessions, governed by decree
(based on a law dating back to the First World
War), banned public assemblies, restricted freedom of the press, dissolved the *Schutzbund* on
March 30, 1933, and banned the Socialist May
festival.

In the meantime, the Hitler regime had come
to power in Germany, and the German pressure on
Austria began first on May 29, 1933, with the
imposition of a tax of 1,000 marks for German
tourists visiting Austria—thus damaging the important Austrian tourist industry.

The final conflict between Social Democrats
and conservatives came in 1934. Searches of the
houses of Social Democratic party members in
Linz encountered armed resistance. A general
strike was called. From February 12 to February 15 there was heavy fighting in Vienna and
the provinces. The Social Democratic party was
dissolved, and some of its leaders were arrested;
others fled abroad.

On May 1, 1934, the new constitution of the
corporate Federal State of Austria was published. On May 20 the first in a series of Nazi
terrorist attacks occurred, with bombs exploding in public places. On July 25, 1934, Chancellor Dollfuss was assassinated in his office
in the Ballhausplatz by members of the outlawed
Austrian SS. Nazi uprisings in Carinthia and
Styria were put down during the next five days.

On July 30, 1934, the minister of justice,
Dr. Kurt von Schuschnigg became chancellor.
Italy stood by Austria, as Mussolini was not
yet fully allied with Hitler. On September 27,
1934, England, France, and Italy guaranteed
Austria's independence. On January 7, 1935,

Italy and France concluded a pact for the defense of the independence of Austria.

Engelbert Dollfuss and Kurt Schuschnigg attempted to revive Austrian patriotism and to create a feeling for an Austrian national identity. The First Republic, it was said, had been a state in search of a people. Now Austrianism was emphasized. Austria was a nation of German-speaking people, based on German cultural values, but through the influences of the former multinational empire, it had been molded into something specifically Austrian. Red-white-red, the Austrian national colors, worn as a band in one's buttonhole became the identification of the Austrian patriot—opposed to Anschluss in general and against the Nazi regime in particular. On May 1, 1935, the *Vaterländische Front* ("Fatherland Front") became the only legal political organization. Supportive of the new constitution, it was awarded the monopoly for political assemblies. On April 11, 1936 Schuschnigg ordered the disarmament of the Catholic armed formations, and a month later he introduced compulsory military service. On June 11, 1936, Germany recognized the full sovereignty of Austria. On July 23 a political amnesty for the Nazis was declared. On October 10, 1936, all private military organizations, including the *Heimwehr*, were dissolved. However, the illegal Nazi organizations continued their work by infiltrating the state apparatus, including the Fatherland Front. In September 1936, Mussolini visited Hitler in Germany. On February 4, 1938, Hitler purged his general staff and invited Schuschnigg to visit him in Berchtesgaden on February 12. The traumatic experience of facing a shouting, threatening, irrational Hitler convinced Schuschnigg that only drastic action could mobilize domestic and foreign support for Austrian independence. On February 24, he

addressed the Bundestag (the parliament) in a
rousing speech, defying Hitler publicly. But
even then, he underlined the Germanic element
in the Austrian nation, reminding his audience
that Emperor Francis Joseph I had refused King
Edward VII's attempt to break up the Austrian
alliance with Germany by saying "Sire, I am a
German Prince."

On March 9, Schuschnigg ordered that a referendum be held on March 13. The wording agreed
upon—to which the voters would respond with a
Yes or No—was: "For a free and *German* [empha-
sis supplied] Austria, an independent and social
Austria, a Christian and united Austria; for
peace and employment and for the equality of all
who stand for their people and their nation."

Let me insert here a personal recollection:
In those days I worked as an unpaid consultant
to the information office of the Fatherland
Front. On March 10, some of us assembled in
the office of State Secretary Guido Zernatto,
in charge of the Fatherland Front, to discuss
the forthcoming referendum. Another participant was Dr. Fritz Bock, also a contributor to
this volume. It was clear that contacts with
the leadership of the underground Social Democratic party had resulted in the understanding
that the Socialists would vote for Austrian independence, simply because they were convinced
that the Schuschnigg regime was by far the less-
er evil than incorporation into Hitler Germany.
At that meeting, the experts estimated that at
least 70 percent of the population would vote
Yes—that is for a free, non-Nazi Austria.

Obviously, Hitler knew that too. On March 11
he moved. He forced the resignation of Schuschnigg and his replacement by his Austrian Nazi
agent, Arthur Seyss-Inquart (hanged after the
Nuremberg trials), and he ordered his armed
forces into Austria. The one man who resisted

to the bitter end was Austrian President Wilhelm Miklas, one of the members of the Austrian
Provisional National Assembly, who in 1918 had
voted against making Austria a constituent part
of the German Republic. On March 11, 1938, at
7:50 p.m., Schuschnigg went on the air, told
the Austrians of the German ultimatum, and said:
"...we are yielding to force. Because we are
resolved on no account even at this grave hour,
to spill *German* blood, we have ordered our armed
forces, in the event of an invasion, to withdraw
without resistance, and to await the decisions
of the next few hours. And so I take my leave
of the Austrian people at this hour with a *German* word and a heartfelt wish: May God protect
Austria" (Taylor, p. 363; emphasis supplied).

On March 13, 1938, Austria was incorporated
into the German Reich. Its name became the Ost-
mark. Theodor Innitzer, the cardinal archbishop
of Vienna, known as a progressive priest and
once minister for social affairs, was one of the
first to greet Hitler upon his arrival in Vienna
and he issued an appeal to vote for the Anschluss. Karl Renner—the veteran Socialist
leader who was the first chancellor of the First
Austrian Republic, and after the second World
War was again chancellor and later president of
the Republic—issued a statement declaring that
the Anschluss was a logical historical development.

The notion of a German Austria had not yet
been fully laid to rest. The trauma of 1918,
the economic misery of the twenties and thirties,
the populist and racial slogans of the National
Socialists, together with the surrender policies
of the Western democracies, account for the acceptance of the Anschluss by a rather sizable
minority of Austrians. And abroad the world was
not ready, as Telford Taylor wrote in *Munich:
the Price of Peace*, to face up to unpleasant
realities (p. 1064).

On November 1, 1943, the Allied powers issued the Moscow Declaration, stating that Austria was to be treated as an enemy-occupied country, to be liberated and restored as an independent state.

The Second Austrian Republic was born in May 1945.

A study of the events up to and following 1945 might tell us what lessons can be learned for solutions of some of our contemporary problems.

In February 1862 the German dramatist Friedrich Hebbel wrote (p. 268):

Austria is the little world in which the big world has its rehearsal.

Sources

Bauer, Otto. *The Austrian Revolution.* New York: Burt Franklin, 1925; reprint ed. 1970.

Churchill, Winston S. *The Gathering Storm.* Boston: Houghton Mifflin, Riverside Press, 1948.

Foreign Relations of the United States, 1918. Supplement, Vol. I.

Hebbel, Friedrich. "Prolog zum 26. Februar 1862," in *Sämtliche Werke*, vol. 2. Hannsludwig Geiger, ed. Berlin and Darmstadt: Tempel Verlag, 1961.

Lansing, Robert. *The Peace Negotiations—a Personal Narrative.* Boston and New York: Houghton Mifflin, Riverside Press, 1921.

Lansing, Robert. *War Memoirs.* New York: Bobbs-Merrill Company, 1935.

Schorske, Carl E. *Fin-de-Siècle Vienna: Politics and Culture.* New York: Alfred Knopf, 1980.

Shepherd, Gordon Brook. *The Last Habsburg.*
New York: Weybright & Talley, 1968.

Taylor, Telford. *Munich: The Price of Peace.*
Garden City, N.Y.:   Doubleday, 1979.

MARTIN F. HERZ

Allied Occupation of Austria: The Early Years

First Impressions of Vienna, 1945

I was chosen to be in the lead jeep of the U.S. "reconnaissance party" that came to Vienna on July 22, 1945, to make arrangements for the setting up of headquarters, U.S. Forces, Austria (USFA). I was a major at that time and had been seconded to the headquarters company by the "political division" of USFA—then still located in Verona, Italy—which was the office of the political adviser to Gen. Mark Clark and the precursor of the American legation in Vienna.

On the day after my arrival in Vienna, I had an interview with State Secretary without Portfolio Leopold Figl, who was the equivalent of vice-chancellor in the Soviet-appointed Renner government. That meeting arose by sheer accident, but to his dying day Mr. Figl, who later in 1945 became chancellor of Austria, attributed our encounter on July 23 to extraordinary sagacity on the part of "the American intelligence service, which already then realized that I was destined to become the leader of my country."[1]

It was no accident, however, that I was a member of the political division and that I had been placed in the leading jeep entering Vienna. Although a native American, I had received most of my education in Vienna and could in fact pass for a native of that city. During the war in Europe my field of activity had been psychological warfare against German troops, facilitating

their desertion, surrender, or capture. In that
capacity it had been my special pleasure to write
appeals to troop units made up predominantly of
Austrians, such as the 5th Mountain Division and
the 44th Infantry Division, calling their attention to the Moscow Declaration of 1943, in which
America, Britain, and Russia had announced their
decision that Austria "shall be liberated from
German domination." In Italy in 1943-44 I had
made a specialty of interviewing Austrian de-
serters and other prisoners, trying to gauge the
extent to which the people of Austria still felt
themselves part of the Greater German Reich.

It is perhaps important to emphasize here, in
view of my background and history, that I was not
an emigrant and was not imbued with any particular political or emotional hang-ups with respect
to Austria. I was interested in the country,
felt well qualified to interpret some of its com-
plexities to my superiors, and welcomed being
among the first Americans in Vienna because I
hoped to send reports to Verona about the Renner
government, about which the Western Allies entertained the most serious reservations. So my
first meeting with Figl, which had been a case
of pure serendipity, was followed by another on
July 24 in which I questioned him systematical-
ly about the Renner government and about his own
political beliefs. This in turn was followed by
interviews with other members of the provisional
government, notably with Ernst Fischer, the Communist minister of education. Those interviews
were sandwiched in between my other duties, which
had to do with finding quarters for the American
headquarters and its senior personnel.

The first impressions we Americans got of
Vienna were deeply shocking. We had heard about
the destruction from two teams of Allied generals
who had visited Vienna earlier (June 3 and July
16), but since the Russians had been in occupation

there since April we had somehow expected that
more would have been done in the way of removing rubble and starting reconstruction.

Another thing that struck us was that the few
people who were in the streets would hurry along
and look away from us as if trying not to at-
tract attention. Very few women were to be seen.
Only when people realized that we were Americans
and not Russians did we become surrounded by
persons eager to tell us about their experiences—once they had been assured that the Americans were going to stay as part of the occupation of the capital.

The stories we heard about the behavior of the
Russian "liberating" troops were so terrible
that we at first refused to believe them. They
sounded too much like Nazi propaganda, and how
could we know that we weren't being misled?[2]
Even the record of my conversations with Figl,
as transmitted from Verona to the State Department, contained the notation: "On several occasions he made embarrassing remarks about the
Russians, *which the American officers were careful to parry*. One of his remarks was a predic-
tion that considerable numbers of Viennese would
move from the Soviet zone of the city to other
zones not, it was stated, in order to obtain
larger rations but 'particularly because of personal feelings.'"[3] It must have taken extraordinary sensitivity to interpret such a remark
as "embarrassing," but the notation made in
Verona shows that we were concerned that the
Austrians might try to drive a wedge between the
American and Russian occupation forces—and that
we wanted Washington to know we would resist any
such efforts.

The plain fact was that the Russian troops
(which included a substantial proportion from
Central Asia) had been allowed to go on a ram-
page of raping and looting when they occupied

Vienna, behaving, not in accordance with the
Moscow Declaration—which had referred to "liberation"—but just as they had behaved in Berlin.
For a while, I was skeptical about the tales of
"tens of thousands" of raped women, but I recall
that a well-qualified doctor who had to deal with
the approval of abortions requested by rape victims, explained to me that he had arrived at an
estimate, which he regarded as conservative, that
there must have been 70,000 cases of rape by Red
Army soldiers. As for the looting, it was of
two kinds—by soldiers going from house to house
to take any objects of value or alcoholic spirits
they could find, and the systematic removal by
the occupation forces of machinery and equipment,
some of it vital to the running of the city.
One thing that struck us was that buildings bore
notations in white paint showing whether they
had been ransacked by the Red Army and what unit
had done so.

It is unpleasant to dwell on details of cruel-
ty and bestiality, and in mentioning them my purpose is only to explain the outrage and exasperation of the Viennese, which became a fact of
great political importance. So it must be recalled that among the raped women were some who
were very old or very young; that many of the
victims or intended victims committed suicide;
that Soviet soldiers sometimes butchered animals
in houses and apartments; that the occupation
troops seemed to take delight in relieving themselves on the furniture and carpets of "capi-
talists"; and that many of their actions seemed
to be calculated to humiliate rather than to seek
physical relief or financial gain.

In his report on the first three months of his
administration, Chancellor Karl Renner tried to
deal with this phenomenon as delicately as he
could by writing: "The superficial observer is
inclined to overlook too easily the different

circumstances under which the various provinces
were occupied. In general it can be said that
the eastern provinces, although with the deepest
grief, had to recognize that it was much more
difficult for the Russian soldier to free himself from an urge for revenge after the complete
devastation of an area of his own country that
had been inhabited by perhaps ninety million people, than would be the case with armies of countries that have not seen a single enemy soldier
on their own soil."[4] A colleague of mine in the
legation, Ware Adams, recently recalled in conversation with me that a Russian official with
whom he dealt in Vienna used to remark that "the
Austrians at Stalingrad were among those who
fought the hardest." Clearly, the Russians—and
not only they—had difficulty forgetting that
many Austrians had participated, willingly or
not, in Hitler's invasion of Russia.

*Russian Ambivalence and
the Renner Government*

It is my belief that the Russians came into
Austria without any well-thought-out plan for
the political management of the country. This
belief is based on several considerations: Even
while the city was being subjected to terror and
pillage by Red Army troops—a traumatic experience that can never be effaced and that hurt the
Austrian Communist party terribly—the Red Army
leadership laid wreaths at the monuments of Austrian cultural and other heroes and proclaimed
its benevolence toward the population. While
tens of thousands of Viennese women were being
raped, Marshal F. I. Tolbukhin generously facilitated the early opening of the Vienna opera
(not in its bombed-out building but in the *Theater an der Wien*). It was as if two mutually
contradictory policies were being applied.

Even in his efforts to appeal to the Austrian population as a liberator, Marshal Tolbukhin made an initial gaffe that could be attributed only to a lack of qualified advisors on his staff. In his first proclamation, as his troops were entering Austria, he wrote: "The Red Army stands on the basis of the Moscow Declaration of the Allied Powers of October 1943 about the Independence of Austria. The Red Army will contribute to the reestablishment of the conditions that prevailed in Austria *up to the year 1938*."[5]

Now anyone even remotely familiar with the history of Austria in the 1930s would have known that in 1938, when the country was forcibly incorporated into the German Reich, it was not a democracy but a clerically oriented authoritarian state that had dissolved parliament and was ruling on the basis of a "corporate" constitution, patterned largely after that of Fascist Italy. So the declared intention to set the clock back to 1938 evoked exasperation and disbelief from the Austrian Socialists, whose party (then still called the Social Democratic party) had been outlawed in 1934. The matter never became a political issue, because the Russians clearly had not meant what Tolbukhin had said in the proclamation.

One of the tragedies (from the Russian point of view) and ironies (from the Austrian point of view) was that the Red Army soldiers did not exclude the working-class districts of Vienna from their depredations. In fact, one of the stories going around Vienna was that when they entered apartments in the workers' housing projects constructed by the pre-1934 Socialist administration of Vienna, they would exclaim, "Ah, Kapitalist!" because it was inconceivable to them that anyone who wasn't a capitalist could live in the modest comfort—extravagant by Russian standards—that the Austrian workers had

attained under the Vienna Social Democratic mu-
nicipal administration.

That the Communist party had been damaged by
the behavior of Russian troops, and that Moscow
was concerned about this, was apparent from a
number of indicators even before my arrival in
Vienna. In the State Department records is a
letter written by John G. Erhardt, the political
adviser to General Clark, in which he called attention to a report "obtained from 'a well-
placed Austrian' recently in Vienna" that the
anticipated replacement of Marshal Tolbukhin by
Marshal Konev should not be attributed to the
official reason, viz., that Tolbukhin's Third
Ukrainian Army had by its fighting record earned
early discharge, but rather to the alleged fact
that "Stalin was displeased with *the lack of
discipline among Tolbukhin's troops in their relations with the Viennese.*"[6] The same letter
also reported that a French agent named Lambert,
an Austrian who had been to Vienna recently,
"reported that [the Communist leaders] Koplenig
and Fischer had lost a certain amount of standing with the Soviets because of *their failure,
so far, to muster the expected popular support,*
notably in factory elections in which the Communists polled under ten percent."[7]

The very manner in which the Russians had come
to appoint Dr. Karl Renner chancellor also indicates that they had no well-thought-out plan
for Austria. Renner had come to their attention
when he went to a local Soviet command in Glogg-
nitz, a village south of Vienna, to complain
against the outrages of the Russian soldiery.
After he identified himself as the president of
the last democratically elected parliament of
Austria and as chancellor of the first republican Austrian government after World War I, he
was escorted to a higher headquarters, where he
was asked whether he would be willing to write

an appeal to his countrymen to assist the Red
Army in its fight against the retreating Germans.

Renner, as he recorded in a *Denkschrift* ("me-
morial") published in June 1945,[8] first thought
of calling together the surviving members of the
erstwhile Austrian parliament, and was surprised,
when the Russians brought him to Vienna, to find
that the old political parties—the People's party
(successor of the prewar Christian Social party),
the Socialists (erstwhile Social Democrats), and
the Communists—were already fully organized and
ready to discuss the formation of a coalition.
It is clear from his *Denkschrift* and from other
documentation that the Soviets only gradually
came to think in terms of Renner heading a provisional government, that they gave him to understand that the formation of such a government
would be coordinated with the Western Allies,
and that their main concern was to have a functioning civil authority to which they could
delegate the administration of the part of the
country that was coming under their control.

Ernst Fischer, the Communist minister of education, whom I interviewed on August 2, immediately acknowledged that his party was at that
time "a distinct minority." He added that "*had
the Communists been able to come into Vienna
all ready and organized to take over the city*
and assure order and discipline, they would now
have a majority. As it is, with the entire system of government breaking down...the resulting
anarchy [Fischer used that word on several oc-
casions] harmed the Communists more than others.
It is true that during this anarchy elements of
the population plundered, raped and looted, and
it is also only too true that *during this anarchy the Russian first-line troops were among
the worst offenders*." Even the emergency police,
organized under Communist auspices, Fischer said,

contained many of the lowest criminal elements
of the population, and there were frequent cases
where the very protectors of law and order used
their position to do some looting of their own.
"Gradually, order was brought into the city, and
now such cases were the exception. Nevertheless,
it must be said that the prestige of the Communists has suffered badly and they now have but a
fraction of the popular support."[9]

In a sense, of course, Fischer was trying to
shift some of the blame away from the Red Army,
but he was also, by implication, incriminating
his colleague Franz Honner, the Communist minister of interior who had brought so many party
members into leading positions in the police. I
was impressed with Fischer's relative candor, and
drew attention in my memorandum to his "extremely
honest and idealistic manner of speaking and
pleading." I noted that "he speaks very quietly
but with insistence, giving the impression, however, that he is much more interested that you
understand his point of view than that you share
it. He often qualifies his statements, at times
emphasizing that his is only one way of looking
at a problem, and that policies may be proven
wrong and may have to be changed."[10] We know
today that Fischer, who wrote his political
autobiography[11] after breaking with the Communists over the invasion of Czechoslovakia in 1968,
suffered on many occasions during his political
career from what he saw as a need to close his
eyes to some truths in order to serve what he saw
as larger truths.

In the West, as mentioned earlier, the unilateral Russian creation of the Renner government
had caused the worst misgivings. It seemed hard
to imagine that the seventy-five year old chancellor wasn't a puppet of the Russians. A high
official of the British government remarked to
the American ambassador that he believed "Renner

...was selected merely to give the Government
an air of respectability. A man of his age
could not be expected to take an active part in
the Government. The real work, he concluded,
would be done by young, active Communists."[12]
George Kennan, then our chargè d'affaires in
Moscow, invited attention to

*the significance of the Communist retention of
the portfolio of Minister of the Interior. It
is now established Russian practice to seek as
a first and major objective, in all areas where
they wish to exercise dominant influence, control of the internal administration and police
apparatus, particularly the secret police....
If, therefore, Moscow has contented itself with
only three members of the Austrian Provisional
Government openly designated as Communists, this
should not be taken as an indication that the
Russians would be prepared to accept willingly
a permanent Austrian Government in which they
would not have what they consider a controlling
influence.* [13]

These were, of course, very reasonable suppo-
sitions, but they turned out to be wrong for
several reasons. First, Karl Renner, despite
his age, proved to be not only vigorous but ingenious, courageous, and endowed with a surprising moral ascendancy over his cabinet colleagues,
including the Communists. Second, the rapid
restoration of the socialist and conservative
parties not only kept pace with but quickly over-
shadowed the corresponding activities of the
Communists. Third, and most important, the Russians did not insist that the Communists have
their way in the government and, indeed, the
Communists did not challenge the democratic majority even during the interim period when the
Soviets were the only military force in Vienna.

The best example of this is what happened during cabinet discussion of the adoption of a provisional constitution that involved a return, essentially, to the last democratic constitution of Austria as amended in 1929, a proposal that the Communist ministers vigorously opposed (possibly because they wished to keep open the alternative of a "people's democracy"). Renner "declared that notwithstanding their opposition he regarded the measure as adopted if the minority did not indicate by their resignation that the proposals remained unacceptable to them."[14] Since the Communists refused to resign—and despite the unanimity rule of the provisional government—Renner simply declared that the cabinet had decided in favor of the old constitution. When one considers the many other ways in which this matter could have been handled, which would have led to a government crisis and perhaps intervention by the occupying power, one must marvel at the sang-froid with which Renner faced down such Communist opposition.

It deserves to be added, however, that Communist opposition during this interim period was the exception rather than the rule. Virtually all decisions of the Renner government were indeed taken unanimously, and even in the case of the Ministry of Interior a rule applied whereby under secretaries of the other two parties had a right to hold up decisions of the Communist minister with which they did not agree. This system was later strengthened during the period between the convocation of a provincial conference in September and the national elections in November 1945, in which the Communists were shown to be such a small minority that they lost any plausible claim to a major portfolio in the government.

Nevertheless, during the period from May to November, Honner, the Communist minister of

interior, was able to appoint many of his party
colleagues to leading positions in the police,
notably Dr. Heinz Duermayer as head of the Vienna police. Almost from the beginning, however, there were limits to what the Communists
could do. For instance, even before the Western
Allies arrived in Vienna, the Socialist under
secretary of interior, Oskar Helmer, managed to
get the Russians to agree to recall the seventy-
nine year old Dr. Ignaz Pamer, a former police
president of Vienna, to replace Duermayer.[15]
Although Pamer's authority was limited and the
Communist minister, Honner, then appointed Duermayer to head the newly formed political police
(*Staatspolizei*), the presence of a seasoned professional at least nominally at the head of the
Vienna police meant that by the time the Western Allies arrived during the latter half of
August, the nucleus of a non-Communist police
force was already in existence.

The 1945 Elections

Among the first acts of the Allied Commission
when it was established in Vienna in August
1945—four months after the city had fallen to
the Russians—was approval of a conference of
provincial representatives (*Länderkonferenz*)
that was to give the Renner government an opportunity to secure a nationwide mandate, which
in turn would allow it to hold national elections. As a result of that conference, some ex-
ponents of the Western-occupied provinces entered the government, notably Dr. Karl Gruber
of Tyrol, who became under secretary for foreign
affairs. The *Länderkonferenz*, however, did not
bring the removal of Honner as minister of interior. As Renner explained to General Clark,
"First, insistence on his removal would likely
have embittered the Soviets and, second, it

would have opened the way to agitation and
trouble-breeding demonstrations on the part of
the Austrian Communists."[16] This illustrates
the narrow margin on which the Renner government was operating even after the arrival of
the Western Allies in Vienna.

National elections took place on November 25,
1945, and by all accounts they were completely
free both in the Soviet zone of Austria and
elsewhere. The question is sometimes asked why
the Russians permitted free elections when the
Communists were in such a precarious position,
and the conventional answer is that they did
not expect the Communists to lose so heavily.
This implies, however, that they did realize
that the Communists would poll less than either
of the other two parties. Certainly even the
Communists themselves did not predict that they
would win a plurality. When I saw Ernst Fischer
in October, he forecast that his party would win
between 20 and 25 of the 165 seats in the lower
house, which would have corresponded to a maximum of 15 percent of the vote.[17] According to
State Secretary Adolf Schärf, the Communists
told the Russians they expected 25 percent of
the vote.[18]

I was at the Ministry of Interior during the
night when the results were being posted, and
it soon became apparent that the Communists
would have trouble obtaining even the *Grundmandat*, the "basic" election of a deputy in one
electoral district that would enable them to
take a share of *Reststimmen*, the residual votes
that were apportioned according to the Austrian
electoral law only to parties that had obtained
at least one directly elected deputy. It may
be difficult to credit this in retrospect,
since we know today how bad our relations with
the Russians were to become, but that evening
many of us (American as well as British

observers) were hoping that the Communists would obtain their *Grundmandat* so that they would not be completely excluded from the political process in the National Assembly.   In the event, they squeaked by and managed to obtain 4 seats with 5.4 percent of the vote.   The People's party obtained 85 seats, an absolute majority, and the Socialists, 76 seats.[19]

A few days after the elections I was entrusted with a "delicate mission" by C. W. Gray, the counselor of the Political Adviser's office.   I was to seek out Figl, who as leader of the victorious People's party was the chancellor-designate, and tell him that I "had heard people in the Political Adviser's office express the opinion" that the interests of Austria would be best served by maintaining the coalition, including (reduced) Communist participation, even after the People's Party victory.   Figl didn't need convincing, nor did the others.   But the Communists lost the Ministry of Interior and had to content themselves with a minor cabinet position.

I have always wondered why my instructions were cast in such tentative terms, and have come to the conclusion that it had more to do with the personality of the old-style diplomatic officer who gave them to me than with the State Department's instructions, which have meanwhile been published and were quite clear: "...suggest, in your discretion, to party leaders that coalition government should be maintained, at least until the end of military occupation, and Communist representation should be retained in cabinet, in order to facilitate good relations among four powers and to avoid impression that Volkspartei victory automatically means anti-Soviet or anti-Communist policy."[20]   There was no American gloating over the fact that the Austrian conservatives had gained an absolute

majority. On the contrary, it was treated almost as a problem—and it would have been a problem if the People's Party had not realized that
it had more to gain from maintaining the coalition, especially with the Socialists, than from
attempting to govern alone, which would have
placed the Socialists together with the Communists in an opposition role.

Inter-Allied Relations—Political

I have not said much yet about the deterioration in relations between the Western Allies and
the Soviet representatives in Vienna. This is
because in my opinion it was Soviet economic,
rather than political, policy in Austria that
brought about that deterioration. It is true
that there were frictions in the relationship
on the political level also, but during the first
months of the occupation relations were basically cordial—once the difficulties about establishing the various zones and sectors had been ironed
out. While it would be an exaggeration to say
that formal relations were friendly, there was
also informal discussion and even some social
entertaining, including informal lunches and
dinners in which civilians of the Soviet element
of the Allied Commission participated. General
Clark has expressed the opinion that the November 1945 elections marked the real end of anything other than pretended collaboration by the
Russians and goes on to say that soon afterwards
they began both to restrict the freedom of the
Austrian authorities in the Soviet Zone and to
give members of the Communist Party greater
privileges.[21] There is no doubt that there was
a cooling of relations after the 1945 elections
and especially as 1946 wore on, but I believe
this was a relatively slow trend that is better
explained by Soviet disappointment over the

frustration of their economic, rather than their political, aims.

Political points of friction existed in connection with the precarious Western access to Vienna, across Russian-held territory. In January 1946, General Clark ordered military police to prevent Soviet personnel from boarding the American train (the Mozart Express) that linked Vienna and Salzburg. When several Soviet officers and men nevertheless forced their way into the train at the demarcation line, and after they had refused to leave, an American MP killed one of the officers and wounded another. Although Marshal Konev demanded that the sergeant responsible be punished, he was acquitted by a military court on the grounds that he was performing his duty.[22]

In Vienna one important point of friction was the abduction of Austrians and exiles from Eastern Europe by Soviet security services. Some were strong-armed into waiting cars, and one case that is vivid in my memory involved an Eastern European refugee being rolled up in a carpet and tossed into a truck. One day while I was in Vienna a Russian was caught in the act of trying to abduct someone in the American sector of the city. The four-power military police were called, and the Russian was put aboard their jeep. The Russian member of the patrol said the jeep was to proceed to his *Kommandatura*, but the American driver said no, he would be taken to the international MP headquarters. Thereupon the Russian pulled his pistol and put it to the head of the American; whereupon the British member of the four-power patrol pulled *his* pistol and pointed it at the head of the Russian; and it was in this configuration that the vehicle rolled into the courtyard of the Auersperg Palais, the quadripartite police headquarters, where the situation

was disentangled. In retrospect, the remarkable
thing about this episode is not that it occurred,
but that there existed a functioning four-power
military police unit in Vienna.

By far the most important political development in the four-power occupation of Austria
during the period immediately after the November 1945 elections was the negotiation of a new
Control Agreement. It seemed reasonable that
once a nationally elected Austrian government
existed, it should no longer be required to subject its laws to the veto of any of the four occupying powers, as the original Control Agreement had specified. An American proposal, worked
out by First Secretary Ware Adams and first tried
out very tentatively on an informal basis, envisaged that a new Control Agreement should permit Austrian laws (except for fundamental laws
of a constitutional nature) to go into effect
unless they were disapproved by the council.
This was a reasonable proposal, but would the
Russians be willing to go along? Instead of having a veto over Austrian legislation, there
would be a "reverse veto" under the new proposal,
by which any of the Western Allies could *prevent
the council from disapproving* Austrian legislation, which would go into effect, thirty-one days
after submission, unless unanimously disapproved.

This proposal for a revised Control Agreement
was negotiated over five months, in the first
half of 1946. Since the Russians did approve
the reverse-veto principle, there has been much
speculation that somehow they did not know what
they were approving.[23] However, the principal
American negotiator (on the working level) in-
sists that the Russians did not by any means go
along by inadvertence. The draft, he wrote, "did
not slide through unnoticed as many Westerners
later thought must have happened, on the theory
that the Soviet Government would never enter into

an agreement which seemed so desirable from our
point of view. Actually, every word of it came
under close scrutiny. Article 6-A (the 'negative veto') in particular was the special subject
of repeated discussions in the Allied Council,
the Executive Committee, and the Political Directorate, as well as the four political divisions
of military government, with a searching question-
ing of it on behalf of the Government in Moscow."[24]

In fact, when the agreement was sent to the
governments for final approval, it was the Soviet
high commissioner who first received the green
light from Moscow. Then followed London and
Paris in due course, but there was still no word
from Washington. In June 1946, the State Department cabled that it was prepared to go along "*despite serious misgivings concerning Article
6-A,*"[25] but thought the matter should await the
outcome of the Council of Foreign Ministers.
There is little doubt that in Washington the fact
that the Russians had approved the new agreement
made officials acutely uncomfortable. As Adams
put it, "Many Americans in those days, including
bureaucrats, had a deep-seated, instinctive view
(often explicitly stated with almost religious
conviction) that anything good for the Communists must ipso facto be bad for us and vice
versa."[26] Finally, American approval was tele-
graphed when it was pointed out by the Political
Adviser in Vienna that a certain Austrian law
having to do with restitution of property, which
was a matter of some political sensitivity in
the United States, might run afoul of a Russian
veto if it was submitted to the Allied Council
while the old Control Agreement was still in
force.[27]

I prefer not to speculate as to why the Russians deliberately weakened their hold on the
Austrian government in this manner. It is

certain that they came to regret their approval
of the new Control Agreement, especially in connection with their disputes with the Austrians
and the Western Allies over the matter of German
assets in Eastern Austria. Adams believes that,
seeing America's role in Austria growing, the
Soviets signed the more liberal agreement because they thought that although it would lessen
their own influence on the Austrian government,
the same would be true of American influence
("We wanted to get the Russians out of Austria;
the Russians equally wanted to get the Americans
out of Austria").[28] It is possible that the
Russians had no *political* master plan for Austria—beyond keeping the country separate from
Germany. But they knew precisely what they
wanted out of Austria in the economic field.

Inter-Allied Relations—Economic

We now return to the beginning of the story,
the early and middle part of 1945. At the time
when they entered Austria, the Soviets based
themselves publicly on the Moscow Declaration of
1943, which had identified Austria as a country
to be "liberated from German domination." However, it became known publicly only much later
that at Moscow in 1943 the Soviet Union had
pressed for insertion of a clause saddling Austria squarely with "full political *and material*
responsibility for the war."[29] This had been at
once contested by the British and American delegates as being manifestly inconsistent with the
declared aim of the powers to treat Austria as
a victim of aggression. They had argued that
not only had Austria ceased to exist as a state
after the annexation in 1938—and could not
therefore have been responsible in any way for
Hitler's actions in 1939 and afterwards—but that
to speak of "material" responsibility implied

that she would be subject to claims for reparations; and demands for reparations would hardly square with a professed desire to reestablish Austrian independence. In the face of Russian obduracy, the Western Allies agreed to add a phrase to the Moscow Declaration that read: "Austria is reminded, however, that she has a responsibility which she cannot evade, for participation in the war on the side of Hitlerite Germany, and that in the final settlement, account will inevitably be taken of her own contribution to her liberation."[30]

I had interpreted this sentence as a psychological device to encourage the Austrian people to be more active in opposition to the Nazis; but to the Russians, obviously, the important clause was the one speaking of "a responsibility which she cannot evade," and agreement on that principle gave a certain plausibility to their position at the Potsdam conference where they reiterated their claim for reparations from Austria. It must be remembered that at the time of Potsdam the Western Allies were not yet in Vienna, and the Russians were already dismantling industrial equipment in Eastern Austria under their definition of "war booty."[31] Molotov at Potsdam proposed that reparations from Austria should be fixed at $250 million, payable in goods over a six-year period.[32] This was at once rejected by both the British and American representatives as being incompatible with the Allied pledge in the Moscow Declaration to treat Austria as a liberated country, and Secretary of State Byrnes later pointed out that Austria would require Western assistance through the United Nations Relief and Rehabilitation Administration (UNRRA). The Western powers proceeded from the realization that if Russia continued to remove assets from Austria while that country was receiving aid

from the West, this meant in a sense that the
West would be indirectly helping to finance Russia's reconstruction without any quid-pro-quo.
I believe that this is precisely what the Russians wanted in Austria, and it is also what
they got.

Having failed to win approval for Austrian
reparations, the Soviet Union managed to obtain
Allied agreement at Potsdam that they could
satisfy their desire for reparations from Germany by seizing appropriate German foreign assets "in Bulgaria, Finland, Hungary, Roumania
and Eastern Austria."[33] There was no longer any
mention of reparations from Austria, but the effect was to be the same. As one commentator put
it: "the provision concerning Austria left room
for very wide interpretation, and the Soviet
Government did not hesitate to apply it in the
following months and years to justify *seizures
in eastern Austria which would never have been
contemplated for a moment by either the British
or the Americans, had they realized what was intended.* The issue was to become a central one
in future discussions of the Austrian Treaty,
and the initial failure to resolve it was to
place a millstone around the neck of the Austrian economy for the next ten years."[34] The fact
is, however, that the West did agree that German
assets in Eastern Austria belonged to the USSR.
Henceforth, the controversy was over the question of what was a reasonable definition of such
assets.

When the Renner government issued its first
proclamation to the Austrian people, the Communists insisted that it include a reference to the
clause of the Moscow Declaration reminding Austria that it had "a responsibility which she cannot evade." That reference was coupled with a
declaration of the willingness of the new government to do what it could to assist the Red Army,

"although that contribution, regrettably, can only be limited in view of the enfeebled and dispossessed condition of our country."[35]

Believing myself that pursuant to the Moscow Declaration the future status of Austria might be judged in accordance with an appraisal of its efforts to contribute to its own liberation, I drafted a dispatch in October entitled "Anti-Nazi Resistance in Vienna from 1938 to 1945."[36] It was forwarded to Washington together with my personal evaluation that the lack of foreign assistance and day-to-day encouragement, the great physical difficulties of underground organization in Austria (for instance due to the common language and the existence of a substantial minority of Austrians who considered themselves to be Germans), and the lack of arms and other physical means of resistance, combined to make the efforts in Vienna much more respectable than might appear from mere comparison between the Austrian effort and that of the occupied countries in the West. In view of those differences and handicaps, I concluded, the resistance efforts I had analyzed, although not important in military terms, possessed "great political significance."

That report did not create any particular reaction in Washington, which is not surprising since it supported a position that, unknown to me, the United States had already taken some time before, in the European Advisory Commission, where the Russians had asserted that Austria's relatively small contribution to its liberation justified their economic claims. According to a telegram from the secretary of state in April, it was the U.S. position that "although in our propaganda we have consistently exhorted the Austrians to 'contribute to their own liberation' we do not believe that they can be judged at this time to have failed

to do so...considering the grip held by the Ge-
stapo and the meager aid from outside up to the
entry of the Red Army into Austria this month."[37]

It is not necessary for the purpose of this narrative to go into great detail with respect to
the Russian removal of industrial equipment from
Austria, their seizures of the oil fields and the
Danube Shipping Company, and the establishment of
a "state within a state" in the form of their administration of some 200 allegedly German properties in Austria. The inter-Allied discussions of
the subject of German assets were prolonged, sometimes acrimonious, and for a long time inconclu-
sive—except for a brief period in 1949 when the
Soviets seemed to fall in with a French proposal
that envisaged a cash payment to the USSR in return for its relinquishment of most, though not
all, of its claims.

The Western position included some excellent
arguments—for instance, reference to the declaration of the United Nations of January 5, 1943,
which had reserved the right to declare invalid
any transfers of property in occupied territories,
whether such transfers had taken the form of
"open looting or plunder, or of transactions apparently legal in form, even when they purport
to have been voluntarily effected." It was also
pointed out that the Russian actions, by handi-
capping the recovery of Austria, were clearly in
contradiction to the spirit of the Moscow Declaration, which had spoken of "opening the way for
the Austrian people...to find that political
and economic security which is the only basis
for lasting peace."[38] The West also was able to
point out that according to the Potsdam Agreement, Russian reparations claims (against Germany) were to be satisfied from "appropriate"
German external assets, which implied that not
every property that was nominally German at the
end of the war was necessarily really a German

asset. But the Russians had physical possession
of the disputed properties, which put them in a
rather strong position.

While the aims of the Soviet Union with respect to the claimed German assets in Austria
were clear, the methods that were pursued were
different at various times. The policy at first
was to remove industrial plants physically from
Austria, but after a while it was found that
this method was inherently inefficient. (Removal of rolling stock and other readily movable
equipment continued, however.) Shortly after
Potsdam, the Soviets proposed that their holdings of alleged German assets be taken over by
Soviet-Austrian joint stock companies. For instance, the Soviets proposed the formation of a
joint oil company, valuing their possession of
oil properties and exploration rights at $13.5
million and Austrian assets at only $500,000.
The Austrians were to be given five years in
which to raise their full share in cash (in
U.S. dollars) to complete their half of the in-
vestment. Since some of the oil properties had
originally belonged to Standard Oil of New Jer-
sey, and the Socony Vacuum Company, the United
States immediately warned the Renner government
against entering any such arrangement, "pointing out that it would have a most unfortunate
effect at the present time when assistance to
Austria from abroad is so greatly needed."[39]

In the spring of 1946 the Soviet Union suddenly abandoned its policy of wholesale removals from Austria and adopted a new plan whereby
most of the remaining "German assets" were formally placed under a Russian trust and were set
to work producing goods for Russia. The economic administration that was developed was
called USIA (Administration of Soviet Property
in Austria) and came to control enterprises
producing such commodities as oil, sulphuric

acid, rayon, sheet metal, electrical equipment,
building materials, and glass. There were also
large agricultural holdings. USIA was totally
divorced from Austrian law and engaged in ex-
porting, importing, and sometimes selling domes-
tically without regard to Austrian official controls, and even in some instances paying wages
(to Communists) that far exceeded the Austrian
wage guidelines. Moreover, USIA developed armed
brigades (called *Werkschutz*) for the protection
of its plants, which had ominous implications
for the stability of the government, particularly since the Austrian law-enforcement establishment was very poorly armed.[40]

The question of dates now becomes important.
The new Control Agreement was signed by the four
powers in Vienna on June 28, 1946. On June 27,
one day before that signature, TASS reported
that the Soviet Union had issued a directive
(order no. 17) transferring all German property
in Eastern Austria to the ownership of the USSR.
The Western powers immediately protested this
order, and General Clark in a letter to his Russian counterpart noted that:

*no definition of German property is given. I
feel this is unfortunate, since it leaves unsettled the important question of whether Austrian property seized by Germany in Eastern Austria after the Anschluss is to revert to Austrian control....I assure you that my Government ad-
heres fully to the decision of the Potsdam conference providing that no reparations should be
exacted from Austria; that Allied claims to German reparations should be satisfied in part from
appropriate German external assets....According-
ly, my Government has never questioned the right
of the USSR to take over possession and ownership
of bona fide German assets located in Eastern
Austria. However, cases have arisen in which*

*the Soviet authorities have cited the Potsdam
Agreement as authority for the seizures of property which had been taken from former Austrian
owners by the German Government or German Na-
tionals by forced transfer during the period of
German control of Austrua.* [41]

The Austrian government was up in arms over
the Soviet order. The parliament passed a resolution challenging its validity, and on July
10 the U.S. high commissioner publicly took the
same position. On July 11, Chancellor Figl at
a special session of the lower house rejected
the Soviet order and recalled the Allied wartime
declarations that had pronounced the forced
transfers of property in Nazi-occupied countries
null and void. It is interesting to note that
Ernst Fischer, whom we have encountered earlier
as Communist minister of education and who was
now one of the party's four deputies in the
lower house, tried to justify the Soviet action
by claiming that the Soviets had "delayed the
execution of the Potsdam Agreement longer in
Austria than in other countries" and that if the
Austrian government had been willing to negotiate directly with the USSR, instead of leaving the matter for resolution between the occupying powers, it "could have had a favorable
interpretation."[42] He was shouted down by the
People's Party and Socialist deputies.
On July 26, 1946, the Austrian parliament en-
acted a long-pending law nationalizing the
largest banks; the coal, lead, copper, iron, and
antimony mining industries; the oil and steel
and certain machine and metal industries; electrical and automotive plants; the Danube Shipping Company; and some power installations and
transportation firms. Of the over seventy
enterprises involved, nearly half were under
Soviet control.[43] As soon as the law came before the Allied Council, Col. Gen. L. V. Kurasov,

the Soviet representative, protested that it in-
terfered with the right of the Soviet Union to
dispose of German property in accordance with
previous Allied agreements. It was pointed out
to him, however, that the law was not a "constitutional" one, which under the new Control Agreement required approval of the council. Whereupon
Kurasov declared that the Soviets reserved the
right to take such steps as seemed to them necessary for the protection of their interests in the
Soviet zone. In view of the fact that the law
would obviously not be permitted to go into effect in that zone, the Austrian government suspended its application for the duration of the
occupation.

The Situation as of the Second Half of 1946

Although the lamentable story of the dispute
over "German assets" did not by any means end
with this episode, it is time to look at the
situation in Austria in its entirety and to place
the political and economic factors in perspective. If any point can be identified when a
"Cold War" broke out between the USSR and the
Western Allies in Austria, it probably was *not*
after the elections of November 1945 (although
some cooling of relations became noticeable after
that event), but was instead after the Russians
came to an open confrontation with the Austrians
and the Western occupation powers over the issue of German assets in mid-1946. As one chroni-
cler reported: "The Soviets, who undoubtedly
felt that the Americans and British at Potsdam
had given them a blank check on 'external German assets,' obviously resented [the] American
attempt to 'cancel payment' on the check....
The lines were now drawn. The policy differences which had been steadily increasing had now
produced a clear, public split in the Allied
occupation."[44]

On August 29, 1946, the United States political adviser in Vienna reported to the secretary
of state:

*Russians now beginning to feel new control agree-
ment of 28 June is tending to let power in Austria slip from their hands....Soviet AC [Allied
Council] member introduced six various resolutions all tending to nullify new control agreement by instructing Austrian Government not to
implement it until instructed to do so by (unanimous) instructions from AC. All six were vetoed
by western elements....New control machinery thus
strengthens Austrian Government as well as western influence in AC. However, an unfortunate
corollary will be increased reluctance of Soviets
to withdraw forces from Austria as long as Potsdam questions are unsettled and they must rely
upon occupation forces to enforce their claims
to disputed German assets.*[45]

A dispatch later that year characterizing the
situation of the various occupying powers, noted
that "on October 24, a Soviet diplomatic spokesman in Vienna charged the Western Allies with
failure to have a full or sympathetic understanding of Russia's position in Austria. He especially charged the United States with carrying
on a propaganda campaign to present the United
States as a 'ready-to-help angel' and the Soviet
as a 'devil stripping the land.' The Russian
spokesman could hardly have expressed more succinctly a widely held Austrian viewpoint in regard to the policies being pursued by these two
of the four occupying powers."[46]

Conclusions

I am on record elsewhere as stating that the
cold war really began just about when World

War II ended, between the Yalta and Potsdam conferences, because of the disagreements over Russian policies in Eastern Europe—which in turn
were due to the ambiguities in the documents
drawn up in Yalta (for instance, the one on Poland and the Declaration on Liberated Europe)
and the unwillingness of the United States to
have spheres of influence established anywhere
in the world (except in Latin America).[47] It
would fit in with that general conception if,
after reviewing the events in Austria in 1945
and 1946, I were to come to the same conclusion
with respect to the clash between the policies
and interests of the USSR and the United States
in that country. However, my conclusion is that
the cold war did not come to Austria because of
any of the *primary* factors that were in evidence,
for instance, in Germany or Hungary or Bulgaria—
because the Soviet Union pursued different objectives in Austria. Nor did the conflict come
into the open at the same time. As indicated,
I think it came into the open only in 1946.

I have tried to show that in my opinion the
Soviets did not come to Austria with a clear
political plan, but that their economic objectives—to draw as much substance out of Eastern
Austria as possible—had already become apparent
in Moscow in 1943, were reflected in inter-Allied
discussions in early 1945, and were confirmed in
Potsdam in July 1945. I do not believe these
Soviet objectives had the direct purpose of harm-
ing Austria, but rather had to do with the needs
of the Russian economy. The terrible destruction that the Soviet Union had suffered during
the war and its inability to find the necessary
resources for reconstruction—whether from German
reparations or from external loans—accounted
more for their behavior in Austria in the early
years of the occupation than did political considerations of a larger scope.

This is not to say that the events in Austria
unfolded in isolation from those in neighboring
countries. The Russian actions in Hungary were
watched with growing alarm and consternation in
neighboring Austria. Yugoslav territorial
claims were a factor preventing the Soviets
from concluding an Austrian treaty (at least
until the ejection of Tito from the Cominform
in 1948). Russian fears about a remilitarization of Germany found echoes in the Austrian
situation. The Western powers in Vienna cast
anxious glances at Berlin, where no national
government was operating and where the lines between East and West were much more tightly drawn,
and they worried that Vienna might be cut off
from Western Austria or that the Soviet Union
might proceed to partition Austria at any time.
(There were even some American officials, for-
tunately none in really important positions,
who felt that since partition was "inevitable,"
it was better to have it sooner rather than
later. They may well have had some Russian
counterparts.)

The Allied disagreements over Eastern Europe,
Germany, Greece, and Iran, which became magni-
fied during this period, certainly were also
reflected in the attitudes of the occupying
powers toward each other in Austria. On the
other hand, I can find absolutely nothing in
the record, or in my memory, that would suggest
that the detonation of atomic bombs in Japan
had any effect on attitudes in Vienna, whether
Austrian, Russian, or American. Later, when
Czechoslovakia was taken over and Berlin was
blockaded, we—the Western Allies as well as the
Austrians—did change our basic attitude, because we went through a brief period when we
even doubted that an Austrian treaty would be
desirable. Our position, as well as that of
the USSR, in Austria was thus sometimes

fluctuating. But on the whole our policy was
sound in supporting the freely elected Austrian
government and its claim to a viable national
existence free from foreign interference.

Having said this, I wish to state my opinion,
or speculation, that while it was politically
impossible for us to "ransom" Austria, a deal
along those lines would probably have been acceptable to the USSR in the early years of the
occupation for the very reasons that I have outlined, i.e., because of the apparent primacy of
its economic interest in Austria. The Austrians
and the Western Allies were agreed that the Russian economic claims on Austria had to be resisted, but we would not have needed to pour as
much substance into Austria if we had been willing to pay the Russians to leave their zone.
Of course, the American mood was totally dis-
inclined to even entertain such a deal—although
we came close to it in 1949 when we were discussing the French proposal for a lump-sum
settlement of the German assets issue (with the
payment to be made by Austria), and the Russians
got down to bargaining with the Western Allies
about the sum. Agreement seemed at hand, except for some relatively minor details. It was
a fleeting opportunity, and it was lost because
we did not then realize how fleeting it was.
Within a few months, the Soviet Union refused
to discuss the subject at all, throwing up arti-
ficial objections that indicated it was no
longer interested in a treaty; so the negotiations broke down in 1950, and it took an entire-
ly new constellation of events to revive them
five years later.

There is little reason to doubt that the Soviet
Union would have liked to see the Austrian Communists do well in the 1945 elections, but by
the time those elections took place, the Soviets
should have known from their experience in

Hungary that Communist parties do not do well in
free elections under Soviet occupation. The
Russians certainly supported the Communists in
Austria—with money, printing services, transportation, and by the initial inclusion of a Communist minister of interior in the Renner government. But they did not support them nearly as
much as they did in East Germany, or in other
countries occupied by the Red Army. I believe
the most obvious explanation for the Russian
failure to pull out all the stops in favor of
the Austrian Communists is also probably the cor-
rect one: They did not desire to incorporate
Eastern Austria into their sphere of influence
and control. Perhaps it was regarded as too
small. At any rate the economic purposes of the
Soviet Union in its zone of occupation could be
accomplished without imposing complete political
control over the population.

   Having said this, I should add that the Communists in Austria had unusual difficulties to
contend with: The renaissance of the two large
old political parties—the People's Party and the
Socialists—occurred to an extent and with a rapidity and élan that few had expected. Those
parties were also blessed with leaders who, in
retrospect, appear as men of extraordinary stat-
ure: The elderly Renner, chancellor of the
provisional government and later president, whom
both the Russians and the West initially underestimated; the Socialist vice-chancellor (later
president) Adolf Schärf; and Leopold Figl, first
vice-chancellor, then chancellor, and later foreign minister of the Austrian government. If
any of these men had yielded to the temptation
to resume the pre-1934 internecine fighting between their parties, or if they had slackened
in their opposition to the Communists, or if the
Socialists had yielded to Communist appeals for
"joint action" or to their divisive tactics, the

outcome might well have been different. Yet the
greatest handicap of the Communists, in my opinion, was the behavior of the Red Army when it
first arrived in Austria, which traumatized the
entire country.

Notes

1. The circumstances are really quite unimpor-
tant, but they are amusing. On the evening of
our second day in Vienna, Colonel Smith, the
headquarters commandant, asked me to locate "a
place where we can buy a glass of beer." This
proved a great deal more difficult than I had
thought, and when we saw a number of cars in
front of a house in the Schenkengasse, a small
side street near the federal chancellery, I in-
quired whether the place was perhaps some kind
of restaurant or (black market) bar. It turned
out to be, instead, the headquarters of the
Bauernbund, the Austrian peasant organization
that was the backbone of the People's Party.
The director of the *Bauernbund*, Leopold Figl,
received Colonel Smith and me as if we were a
delegation dispatched to him by General Clark.
The story has been recounted in greater detail
in my article "A Glass of Beer with the Chancellor" in *Foreign Service Journal* 30, no. 7 (July
1953):25.

2. A British survey of the period displays
the same perplexity: "...when they reached Vienna, all three of the Western Allies were be-
sieged with stories of the brutality of the Soviet troops, and it was some time before they
realized that many of these were true, and not,
as they thought at first, the propaganda of Goeb-
bels faithfully echoed by people who wished to
drive a wedge between the victors." Michael
Balfour and John Mair, *Four-Power Control in*

Germany and Austria 1945-1946. In Survey of International Affairs, 1939-1946, issued under the auspices of the Royal Institute of International Affairs (London: Oxford University Press, 1956), p. 318.

3. Verona dispatch to Secretary of State, no. 93, August 3, 1945, in U.S. National Archives, file no. 863.01/8-345. All italics within quotations here and throughout this chapter have been supplied by the author for emphasis and are not in the original documents.

4. Dr. Karl Renner, *Drei Monate Aufbauarbeit der provisorischen Staatsregierung der Republik Österreich* (Vienna: Österreichische Staatsdruckerei, 1945), pp. 8-9.

5. *Österreichische Zeitung* (organ of the Red Army in Austria), April 15, 1945.

6. Letter dated July 13, 1945, from John G. Erhardt to H. Freeman Matthews, Director of the Office of European Affairs, Department of State, in U.S. Department of State, *Foreign Relations of the United States, 1945* (Washington, D.C.: Government Printing Office, 1968), 3:568. (This title is hereafter cited as *FRUS*.)

7. The "French agent" Lambert was actually an Austrian resistance fighter by the name of Ernst Lemberger, who later became Austrian ambassador to Belgium, the European communities, and the United States.

8. Karl Renner, *Denkschrift über die Geschichte der Unabhängigkeitserklärung Österreichs* (Zurich: Europa-Verlag, 1946; first published in Vienna in June 1945). I am not unaware of a recent interpretation that considers that Renner's choice by the Russians "was no accident" (Wilfried Aichinger, *Sowjetische Österreichpolitik, 1943-1945* [Vienna: Österr. Gesselschaft für

Zeitgeschichte, 1977], p. 122). This is based
on an article by S. M. Shtemenko in the Soviet
publication *Neue Zeit* alleging that Stalin had
given an order, "in the course of a conversation
in the general headquarters," that it should be
determined whether Renner was still alive, and
if so, where he could be located. It is, of
course, possible that the USSR thought in advance of Renner as the possible head of a provisional government, but on balance it seems
more likely that, as often happens, Soviet historians feel uncomfortable that any important
political action of their government could be attributed to chance.

9. Dispatch, "Memorandum on Conditions in
Vienna," Verona no. 103, August 7, 1945, signed
by John G. Erhardt, Political Adviser, in U.S.
National Archives, file no. 863.00/8-745.

10. Ibid.

11. Ernst Fischer, *Erinnerungen und Reflexionen*
(Hamburg: Rowohlt, 1969).

12. Ambassador Winant to Secretary of State,
telegram 4376, April 30, 1945, in *FRUS, 1945,*
3:101.

13. George Kenna\to Secretary of State, Moscow telegram 1424, April 30, 1945, pp. 105-6.

14. Adolf Schärf, *Zwischen Demokratie und Volks-
demokratie* (Vienna: Verlag der Volksbuchhand-
lung, 1950), p. 18.

15. Balfour and Mair, *Four-Power Control,* p.
362; William Lloyd Stearman, *The Soviet Union
and the Occupation of Austria* (Bonn, Vienna, Zurich: Siegler & Co., 1962), p. 57.

16. Memorandum of conversation transmitted as
Vienna no. 257, October 1, 1945, in *FRUS, 1945,*
3:613-14.

17. Vienna dispatch no. 334, October 18, 1945,
in U.S. National Archives, file no. 863.00/10-
1845.

18. Adolf Schärf, *Österreichs Erneuerung,
1945-1955* (Vienna: Verlag der Wiener Volksbuch-
handlung, 1955), p. 18. Balfour and Mair, *Four-
Power Control*, p. 323, report that the Soviets
expected the Communists to poll 30 percent, which
appears very high.

19. The American political adviser (Erhardt)
in a telegram to Washington on November 27, 1945
(no. 498), reported: "Practically all Communists
are stunned and disillusioned by shattering defeat which was expected by no one, and older
leaders such as Fischer are trying to restore
faith younger party workers." *FRUS, 1945*, 3:665.

20. Telegram no. 329 from Secretary of State
to Political Adviser for Austrian Affairs, December 4, 1945, ibid., p. 674.

21. Mark W. Clark, *Calculated Risk* (New York:
Harper & Brothers, 1950), p. 470. "The Soviets
were both surprised and angered by the failure
of the Communist party to show any strength.
They obviously had been supporting the Austrian
Government in the belief that it would lead to
the establishment of a pro-Communist state; when
they found that the opposite was true, they began to change their attitude toward the Austrian
people."

22. Stearman, *Soviet Union*, p. 37.

23. Balfour and Mair, *Four-Power Control*,
p. 328: "The Soviet authorities' attitude caused
some surprise at the time, and indeed it was conjectured that they might have signed the new
Agreement without fully realizing its implications....It may be that the full implication was
only tardily realized in Moscow, though that

seems unlikely." Stearman (*Soviet Union*, p. 41)
wrote: "It soon became obvious that the Soviets
had unwittingly [*sic*] signed away their strong-
est hold over the Austrian government." He considered it a "plausible explanation" that Russian approval came from "a combination of poor
coordination and an ignorance of Western legal
terminology and norms" (p. 44).

24. Ware Adams, "The Miracle of Austria—a Diplomatic Success Story," *Foreign Service Journal*
48, no. 6 (June 1971):26.

25. Secretary of State telegram no. 543 to
Political Adviser for Austria (Erhardt), June 11,
1946, in *FRUS, 1946*, 5:349.

26. Adams, "Miracle of Austria," p. 26.

27. Ibid.

28. Ibid., p. 27.

29. Balfour and Mair, *Four-Power Control*, p. 279.

30. *FRUS, 1943*, 1:761.

31. Learning of Russian removals of "German"
equipment from Austria, the British government
on April 21 sent instructions to its chargé
d'affaires in Moscow to state: "HMG are sure
that the Soviet Government will agree that our
common purpose might be prejudiced by unilateral
action on the part of any occupying powers in
regard to the removal of industrial plant and
equipment regardless of whether or not this was
German owned." *FRUS, 1945*, 3:82. The United
States made parallel representations, and on
April 25 Kennan reported that they had been rejected by Vyshinsky, who stated that "the Soviet
Government considers that no obstacles should be
placed in the way of the urgent removal of tro-
phy equipment which might be used in the war
against Germany" (ibid., pp. 93-94).

32. *FRUS, The Conference of Berlin (Potsdam),
1945*, 2:323, 666.

33. Ibid., Protocol of the Proceedings, vol. 2,
paras. 8 and 9, pp. 1486-87.

34. Balfour and Mair, *Four-Power Control*,
p. 311.

35. Renner, *Denkschrift*, p. 74.

36. Vienna dispatch no. 337 of October 18,
1945, in U.S. National Archives, file no. 863.00/
10-1845.

37. Secretary of State instruction to John G.
Winant (U.S. representative on the European Advisory Commission), April 10, 1945, in *FRUS,
1945*, 3:58.

38. *FRUS, 1943*, 1:443-44, 761.

39. Vienna telegram no. 165 of September 4,
1945, in U.S. National Archives, file no. 863.
5034/9-445, containing a report of advice by
Erhardt to General Clark on what might be said
to the Austrians. The implication was clear
that if Austria expected to receive American aid,
it had better refrain from any action prejudic-
ing American rights to property that had been
expropriated by Germany during the war.

40. A report in 1948 noted that at that time
only one out of seven policemen in Vienna had
a firearm. Winifred Hadsel, "Austria Under Allied Occupation," *Foreign Policy Reports* 24,
no. 12 (November 1, 1948):137.

41. United States Military Commissioner in
Austria (Clark) to Commander-in-Chief of the
Soviet Central Group Troops (Kurasov), in *FRUS,
1946*, 5:354. Clark protested against the reported order.

42. Vienna press telegram to Department of State of July 12, 1946, in U.S. National Archives, file no. 740.00119, Control (Austria) 7-1246.

43. Hadsel, "Austria," p. 140; Balfour and Mair, *Four-Power Control*, p. 352.

44. Stearman, *Soviet Union*, p. 47.

45. Vienna no. 1184 to Secretary of State, August 29, 1946, in *FRUS, 1946*, 5:363-64.

46. Vienna dispatch no. 2079 of November 27, 1946, ibid., p. 377.

47. Martin F. Herz, *Beginnings of the Cold War* (Bloomington: Indiana University Press, 1966; paperback ed., New York: McGraw-Hill, 1969), p. 188.

The Allied Commission
for Austria

The first Austrian Control Agreement was signed
by the three-power European Advisory Commission
in London on July 4, 1945. The EAC agreement
of July 9, 1945, provided for the division of
Austria and Vienna into occupation zones. On
August 23, 1945, Western forces officially entered Vienna. Just prior to this latter event,
a U.S. advance group, under the command of the
U.S. deputy commander in Austria, Maj. Gen. Al
Gruenther, met with the Soviet authorities to
specifically delineate the U.S. sector, to re-
connoiter for accommodations, and most important to arrange with the Russians for rights of
access to the city. He was accompanied by British and French representatives. Displaying the
bonhomie of the victors, the Soviet military
commander assured the Western delegations that
in the spirit of the Grand Alliance there would
be no obstacles and suggested that such details
could be finalized later. Gruenther persisted,
stating that the U.S. high commissioner and
commanding general, Mark W. Clark, would not
move his headquarters to Vienna from Salzburg
until a written agreement was signed. This was
done, to the annoyance of the Russians—an air-
tight access agreement covering air, road, and
rail transit rights that was later to so dramatically differentiate between Vienna and Berlin. A supplementary local protocol actually
gave the U.S. control of that part of the

Wienerwald beyond the eighteenth and nineteenth
districts "for walking purposes." This too was
later of near-critical importance at the time
of the Berlin blockade.

The U.S. military government team for Austria
had been assembled two years before, a disparate
group of specialists containing some men of truly
remarkable capabilities. This team studied and
trained in the U.S., in London, and in Caserta,
Italy, waiting eagerly for the opportunity to
perform their mission. It assembled briefly in
Verona, Italy, at the headquarters of the 15th
Army Group and then moved to Salzburg until their
entry into Vienna. In contrast to the prolonged
preparation of this group, government of the U.S.
zone of Austria at the local level was initially
performed by young combat officers seconded from
the combat units with no preparation whatsoever.
To the lasting credit of our army, these officers,
who had no axes to grind other than getting home
as soon as possible, performed their duties with
justice, wisdom, and practicality, a feat little
remembered today.

The Allied Commission was organized into directorates, each with representatives of the four
powers: Internal Affairs, Political, Legal,
Finance, Education, Social Administration, Economics, and Transportation and Communications—
corresponding to the equivalent ministries of
the Austrian government-to-be. In addition,
there were five directorates without an Austrian
counterpart: Reparations, Deliveries and Restitution; Prisoner of War and Displaced Persons; Military; Naval; and Air. A four-power
Allied secretariat was established in the House
of Industry on Schwarzenbergplatz. The city
was divided into four sectors, plus an international sector, the First District, and the Vienna Inter-Allied Command (VIAC) was formed to
govern the city.

Heading the Allied Commission was the Allied Council (AC) composed of the four commanders-in-chief, designated as high commissioners. The four deputies made up the Executive Committee (EC). The two bodies met on alternate Fridays. Business items could be placed on the agenda by any power, at any level, i.e., the directorates, the Executive Committee, or the Allied Council. Communications from the Austrian government could likewise be introduced at any level. Normally, business items were first referred to the appropriate directorate by the Allied secretariat.

If there was unanimous agreement in the directorate, the matter was referred to the Executive Committee for ratification (although in some instances the decisions were dispatched directly by the directorate). Items on which there was disagreement could be referred to the next higher level, held over, or dropped. If the supreme body, the Allied Council, could not resolve the question, it could be unanimously referred back for additional examination, or dropped in disagreement. The Allied Council developed a rule that unresolved items would not be made public so long as they were still under study. Chairmanship of the Allied Commission bodies, as well as that of VIAC and control of the First District, rotated monthly, e.g., the U.S. was in the chair in January, May, and September.

The first Allied Council meeting took place September 11, 1945. Not unexpectedly, the initial interests of the Allied Commission extended deeply into the operational affairs of the newly created Republic. As the Austrian government developed its capacity to govern, authority was increasingly vested in its organs. By the end of its ten-year life, only the most vestigial and thoroughly controversial matters remained on the agenda of the Allied Council.

But in the first few years, thousands of business items were taken up by the Allied Council
and its Executive Committee; an index organized
by the U.S. element of the Allied Council shows
ninety-nine *categories* of subjects! Despite the
East-West conflict that dominated the work of
the Commission, there did develop quite apart a
modest, albeit largely unspoken, pride among the
four power staffs that this body was able to
weather such world crises as the Berlin blockade,
the dissolution of the Allied Control Council in
Berlin, the Korean War, and the cold war, and to
go on about its given task of establishing a
free and independent Austria.

There were, nevertheless, moments when its
seeming fragility was tested and the continued
existence of the Allied Commission seemed in
doubt. In February 1947 the Soviet deputy commissioner, together with his advisors, withdrew
from the Executive Committee meeting during an
especially contentious and acrimonious debate.
Four months later, Soviet High Commissioner
Kurasov, unquestionably acting on instructions,
staged a similar walkout. No one knew at that
moment whether or not this signified the end of
four-power rule and the partition of Austria.

When the Soviets clamped down their blockade
on Berlin, the Soviet high commissioner in Austria apparently received similar instructions.
Soviet troops blocked traffic to and from Vienna. General Keyes, the U.S. high commissioner,
went to General Kurasov and made a frank pres-
entation, pointing out the difference between
the Austrian and German situations. Meanwhile,
some engineers and I went up in the area of the
U.S. "walking zone" to select a location for
crash construction of an airfield for resupply
purposes. (Ironically, the U.S. headquarters
had lost its copy of the agreement ceding this
area of the Soviet zone to the U.S., but

evidently the Soviets still had theirs, since
they didn't interfere.)   Whether because of
General Keyes's intervention or for some other
reason, the Russians lifted their blockade after
twenty-four hours.   However, the U.S. authorities subsequently warehoused vast supplies of
food—sufficient to feed the city for some months—
until 1953.

The USSR of course always had within its power
the partition of Austria, but it seemed apparent
from the pattern in eastern satellite countries
that it continued to hope for an eventual Communist takeover of the whole country.   Books (if
not libraries) have been written on this subject, and I will not go into it here, but must
add to the list of crises facing the Allied Council what is generally agreed to be the last big
Soviet / Communist push to topple the legitimate
Austrian government.

The end of the war found hunger, despair, destruction, and economic stagnation dominating
the lives of the Austrian people—especially
those in Vienna and the Soviet zone of occupation.   The Allied Council set the calorific food
ration for the populace.   For example, an Allied
Council decision of March 11, 1946, reduced the
individual ration to 1200 calories—for a people
who had been underfed during the later war years
and had starved thereafter.   The U.S. Army quar-
termaster food stocks were released for feeding
the population until they ran out.   The United
Nations Rehabilitation and Relief Agency (UNRRA)
distributed food (largely U.S. supplies) under
Allied Commission supervision.   In 1947 a U.S.-
Austrian Relief Assistance Agreement was signed;
a subsequent Interim Aid Agreement between the
two countries was concluded in January 1948;
and later in the year the U.S. and Austria entered into agreement for four years of Marshall
Plan aid.   All of these assistance acts were

fiercely attacked in the Allied Council by the
Soviets as efforts to "enslave Austria," and the
Soviet high commissioner declared he would not
permit this "violation of sovereignty in his
Zone."

Consequently, the Russians and Austrian Communists saw the opportunity for a takeover based
on popular discontent and hunger slipping through
their fingers. A general strike was called in
September 1950. Demonstrators and rioters were
trucked into Vienna from the Soviet-seized facto-
ries and oil fields of eastern Austria. One hun-
dred thousand of them converged on the chancellor's office in the Ballhausplatz. The Soviets
had maintained the police in a state of disarmament, and on this occasion they froze the movement of police reserves in their sector. Slowly, the police were beaten back in the streets
leading to the chancellery. The chancellor
called on the U.S. high commissioner, whose
period of chairmanship gave him responsibility
for the First District, to send U.S. military
forces. This General Keyes was reluctant to do.
For his very modest troop strength in Vienna
(less than two battalions) to have routed the
rioters, he would have undoubtedly had to resort
to small-arms fire. Whether the Soviet forces,
whose city headquarters was just across the park,
would have remained inactive during such a battle was an open question. Three times the chancellor made his request, and three times General
Keyes deferred his decision (the U.S. had an
agent in the chancellory whose separate reports
estimated that the police could still hold).
Ultimately, the police resistance mounted and
they slowly hammered the crowds back. Within a
matter of hours the Communist effort collapsed
throughout Austria.

The variety of problems dealt with by the Allied Council, the Executive Committee, and the

thirteen directorates is too vast to be summa-
rized here. They ranged broadly through all
governmental fields: civilian supply, communications, denazification, refugees, all aspects
of the economy, education, governmental finance,
internal security, thousands of Austrian laws,
Austrian foreign relations, control of the press,
transportation....To cite one example, the Soviets proposed as soon as the Allied Commission was
formed what seemed to them a normal state of affairs: namely, the imposition of censorship over
all communications. The Western high commissioners, not unfamiliar with wartime censorship,
agreed—expecting the practice to be a temporary
measure while Nazis and war criminals were being
tracked down. However, being a unanimous quadripartite decision, it would take similar unanimity to undo it. But for eight long years a giant
Allied staff of Austrians drearily opened and
read all mail and telegrams to and from Austria,
and all international phone calls had to be
routed through the Schillerplatz exchange in
Vienna so that Allied censors could listen to
the conversations. The purpose of this immense
activity had long since been lost. The U.S.,
British, and French proposed in the Allied Council in March of 1947 that this practice be abolished, but the Soviets vetoed it. Abolition of
censorship was on the agenda thirty-six times
before the Russians finally agreed to it in August 1953.

Students of the occupation period have written
that the Soviets were quite good about abiding
by agreements once they entered into them within
Austria. This is an overstatement. I recall
that at the request of my high commissioner in
1951 I compiled a list of Russian violations of
the Control Agreement. This list, submitted to
the State Department, was quite long. Most of
them consisted of Soviet refusals to permit the

application of various Austrian laws in their zone.

As has been described by other contributors, the Americans, British, and French made early efforts to conclude a peace treaty that would end the occupation of Austria. This was first proposed by the U.S. high commissioner in the Allied Council on February 25, 1946. However, Soviet obstruction of this state treaty (which lasted until ten years after the war) is another story. I served as a member of the U.S. delegation to the Council of Foreign Ministers and of the Deputy Foreign Ministers, as well as with the Austrian Treaty Commission, through most of the meetings until that happy day when the four foreign ministers met in Vienna on May 15, 1955, to sign the treaty making Austria truly independent.

ADOLF STURMTHAL

The Strikes of 1950

Having been revealed as an insignificant political minority by the two first general elections
held after the defeat of the Nazis, the Communists transferred the main emphasis of their actions to the plants, especially to the USIA
(Russian-controlled) plants in the Soviet zone
of Austria. There they had fairly substantial
influence upon large numbers of industrial workers, not a few members of the works' councils,
and some trade union leaders at the medium and
lower levels. The overwhelming majority of the
top union leadership was associated with the
Socialist party. If, nevertheless, the Communist party (CP) had a somewhat disproportionate
influence upon the works' councils, it was due
to the not unreasonable belief of some non-
Communist workers that, at least in the Eastern
zone, a CP council chairman could deal more effectively with management—mostly under CP control—and the Soviet authorities. To shift from
their unsuccessful electoral politics to reli-
ance on economic action that would ultimately
lead to political success was, under the circumstances, a reasonable change in strategy for
the Communists.

The role of the Austrian trade unions in public affairs was greatly strengthened in the
post-World War II era by their organizational
unification. True, this was a somewhat strange
form of unity, since the existence of political
factions within the unified organization was
officially acknowledged and continues to be the

basis for a rough kind of proportional representation in the top leadership of the unions.
As a result, most union leaders are Socialists.

Moreover, the union position was enhanced by
their high degree of centralization and their
new relationship with management. Unlike the
atmosphere during the interwar period, mutual
recognition and respect, rather than distrust
and hostility, prevailed and continues to this
day.

Finally, in resisting a Communist takeover,
the unions had the strong support of public
opinion. Indeed, given the enforced semiparaly-
sis of the state, the unions were the most powerful anti-Communist force in the country.

The Communists had some reasons to hope for
the assistance of the Soviet military authorities; though Soviet faith in the Austrian Communists had been badly shaken by the election
returns and the low prestige of the Communist
leaders—with perhaps one or two exceptions—among
the Austrian workers. The Russians were in the
process of changing their Central European
strategy, given their lack of success in preventing West Germany's military tie-in with the
Western Alliance. Still, the Austrian CP cannot be accused of excessive optimism if they
expected some measure of Soviet support, and to
some degree—probably short of their more extreme
hopes—they received it.

They were further encouraged by two chains of
events: one, the fall of Czechoslovakia; two,
the sharp deterioration of Austria's economic
prospects and the clumsy handling of this issue
by the Socialists.

The Communist takeover in Czechoslovakia in
1948 had created a mood of despair among many
of the neighbors of the Czechoslovak republic.
The shock was serious: Under President Benes,
a predominantly pro-Moscow government had been

formed at the request of the Communists with
Zdenek Fierlinger as prime minister. Fierlinger
was the former Czech ambassador to Moscow, and—
as events rapidly demonstrated—a faithful agent
of the Soviet government. That even this regime
did not please Moscow and had to be replaced by
an openly Communist dictatorship, dealt a severe
blow to the hopes of those who wanted to combine
neutrality with independence. To some observers,
the ultimate takeover of all countries that Soviet troops had reached—and thus possibly a split
of Austria into a Communist and a non-Communist
part—appeared unavoidable.

However, the most promising turn of events from
the CP point of view was the developments sur-
rounding the Fourth Price and Wage Agreement,
concluded at the end of September 1950. It made
possible mass Socialist support for a Communist-
led movement of resistance, and without such non-
Communist support no rebellious movement could
succeed. The role of the Socialist unionists
thus became crucial.

A few words of explanation regarding this
agreement may be necessary. Almost immediately
after the end of the hostilities that had left
Austria economically exhausted and helpless,
changes of prices and wages were under strict
control of a group representing employers, peas-
ants, unions, government, and experts. Their
work had functioned reasonably well, given the
frightful circumstances under which they operated.
This changed with the outbreak of the Korean War
and with the reduction of Marshall Plan aid which
forecast its approaching end.

Korea caused U.S. authorities to engage in
rapid and large-scale purchases of raw materials
to build up strategic storage dumps. This led
to a worldwide wave of price increases, some of
a very substantial nature. Except for the first
three months of 1950, when retail prices in

Austria remained pretty stable, that year wit-
nessed a wholesale price increase of some 10
percent; between mid-June and mid-September
alone, the index of wholesale prices rose by almost 9 percent. This was bound to be reflected
in consumers' prices. At the same time, the reduction of Marshall Plan aid to Austria forced
the government to reduce price subsidies: first,
subsidies of coal and coke; later, and with more
devastating immediate impact, the subsidies on
bread; and to complete the picture of impending
crisis, the peasant organizations, politically
very powerful, asked for increases in grain
prices. Total result: The cost of living increased some 480 points between April 1945 and
October 1950, while wages rose only 337 points.[1]

Negotiations on how to deal with the issue were
understandably difficult and prolonged. The
longer they lasted, the greater the pressure of
the representatives of agriculture: The farmers
refused to supply the urban markets. Public
quarrels broke out among the participants to the
negotiations, while lack of information and a
good deal of misinformation aroused the ire of
the workers. This was fertile soil for Communist propaganda.

The system of high-level negotiations on all
major issues that has been characteristic of
post-World War II Austria has produced many advantages for the population in general and the
working class in particular. Low unemployment
and low rates of inflation combined with rising
living standards have created an atmosphere of
social peace and contentment that, *though not
without serious problems*, is the envy of most
other industrial market economies. But the system was still new in 1950 and did not enjoy the
measure of confidence on the part of the workers
that it had in later years, especially during
the sixties and seventies. Moreover and most

importantly, its successful operation was a function of a rapidly growing national product. In 1950, however, it had to deal with a decline in GNP and the consequent allocation of losses rather than gains. This severe test threatened to reduce the system to shambles and gave the Communists the opportunity for action they had been hoping for.

Every aspect of the compromise that was sprung upon the public in the form of rumors, partly by word of mouth, partly in the press, on September 26—providing for wage and price increases, with the latter, according to the Communists, approximately three times larger—came under a blitz attack. The cost-of-living data were questioned and Chamber of Labor figures about the drop of real wages were cited to indicate the unfairness of the new arrangement, even before the trade unions had an opportunity to evaluate the still-secret agreement in an official statement.

The strike movement sponsored by the CP and started on September 26 proceeded in two phases. The first, though based primarily in the Russian zone, extended rapidly into the West. It centered there on the VÖEST in Linz and Steyr, on the power plant of Kaprun, and on the Alpine Montan works of Donawitz. In Linz striking workers occupied the building of the Chamber of Labor, an unheard-of act of rebellion. Several events gave this strike movement its special character.

First, Socialist workers participated in large numbers, some of them in the belief that because legitimate trade-union leaders had criticized the agreement, they supported the strike. Other non-Communist workers rebelled against the union leaders. The Socialist support was critical for the success of the strike, since the Communists represented such a small minority among the workers.

Second, the participation of so many non-Communist workers in the strike indicated the extent to which communications between the union leaders and the rank and file had broken down. This was the opening for a Communist-designed offensive to drive a wedge between the union leaders and the rank and file.

Third, there was the uncertainty about the intentions of the Soviet authorities. The U.S. was tied up by the highly unfavorable course of military events in Korea and was morally handicapped in the eyes of many workers by their known support of higher agricultural prices. Would the Soviets take advantage of the weakness of their main adversary, and how far would their support go?

Mass support for the strike in Vienna centered in the working-class districts in the Russian-occupied sector of the city: Favoriten, Brigittenau, Floridsdorf. They also contained some of the largest USIA (Russian-controlled) plants. Police forces from these areas could not be used to check the demonstrators, as the Soviet authorities had prohibited their use. Police from the rest of the city was unarmed out of fear that bloodshed would provoke the Soviets into open intervention. Nor were the U.S. authorities willing to intervene, perhaps in the hope of forestalling an armed confrontation between the U.S. and the Soviet Union. Similar restrictions on the use of regular police were imposed on the Austrian authorities as far as Soviet power reached.

In Linz, the conflict centered on the VÖEST (Vereinigte Österreichische Stahlwerke) works, whose works' council was dominated neither by the Socialists nor by the Communists, but by the "Independents," a successor to the Nazi party. A large number of the workers were refugees without much union experience. Like the Vienna

workers in the eastern sector, the VÖEST workers—
though in the U.S. zone—followed the strike pa-
role, as did many workers in Styria. Thus, the
first strike day saw the CP offensive in rapid
advance, having wrested the leadership from the
Socialists, thanks mainly to the failure of the
latter to keep their members informed. Neither
the Linz nor the Graz newspapers had yet published the text of the new agreement.

By the next day, September 27, Socialist leaders and the union officials began to organize
their counteroffensive. Nonetheless, the morn-
ing of that day still brought the occupation of
union headquarters in Linz by CP-led strikers
and the enforced resignation of trade-union leader Heinrich Kandl. In Graz, the capital of
Styria, similar actions occurred. On the next
day, however, the Communist offensive in Vienna
failed miserably. Striking workers, now again
under the discipline of their Socialist union
leaders, returned to work in increasing numbers.

A second wave of strikes followed an unsuccessful ultimatum by an "All-Austrian Works'
Council Conference," held on September 30. The
demand was for either an abolition of the wage-
price agreement or the doubling of the wage increases. No demands for the resignation of union
leaders were made any more. The Austrian Communists in organizing this conference were following on a highly modest scale the model set by
the successful Communist takeover in Prague in
February 1948. However, the threat of the strike
call for October 4 made little impression on the
union leaders, who were aware that only a tiny
fraction of works' council members had attended
the CP-sponsored conference. The Socialists in
turn called a conference of their shop stewards
for October 3, explained the agreement, and organized a large-scale propaganda campaign against
what they described as the threatened takeover
by the Communists.

Once again the Soviet authorities intervened, and in the same fashion as before. The police president of Vienna, Josef Holaubek, one of the pillars of the Viennese Socialist party, was instructed by the Soviet authorities not to use his police forces on the day of the general strike. Similar orders were issued to the police in other parts of the Soviet zone. This left open the question of how much further the Russians would go in assisting their Austrian associates.

On October 4 it soon developed that no serious strike activities were occurring outside the Soviet zone of occupation, and even in Lower Austria only a small fraction of the workers, almost all in USIA plants, followed the strike order. Under the circumstances, the Communists concentrated on blocking traffic, but without lasting success. Their failure was due less to the actions of the police—which, under Russian threats, had refrained from using any weapons— than to the resistance of the workers themselves.

It is at this point that a trade union leader acquired a nationwide reputation. Franz Olah, president of the construction workers union, called upon his members, whose loyalty to him was well-known. He organized them into small troops equipped with the tools of their trade, clubs, pieces of wood, etc. The "Olah battallions" used force against force with considerable success. They destroyed roadblocks all over Vienna, drove away Communist pickets, and cleared the streets where necessary. In Lower Austria similar—though because of the location, less spectacular—battles were fought by the well-organized railroad workers. The resistance of the workers themselves, together with the failure of the Soviet troops to intervene in the conflict (with one exception: the threat of military intervention in the battle for the post office building in Wiener-Neustadt) proved

decisive in what was, in any case, a desperate,
last-ditch effort of the Communists.

The emergence of Franz Olah on the national
scene marked the beginning of a meteoric career
in Austrian politics. Born in 1910 in Vienna,
he joined the Socialist party and the union as
soon as his working life began, i.e., in 1924.
Between 1934 and 1938—the years of the Dollfuss-
Schuschnigg dictatorship—he participated in the
underground activities against the clerico-
fascist regime and spent more than a year and a
half in jail. Arrested again as soon as Hitler
marched into Austria, he was detained for more
than seven years in a concentration camp. Re-
turning home in 1945, he became one of the general secretaries of the Construction and Woodworkers' Union, later, president of the union,
and in 1948, a member of parliament. Five years
after the events of 1950, he became vice-president and four years later president of the Austrian Trade Union Confederation. Early in 1963
he was made Minister of the Interior, an office
he kept for only a year and a half. His forced
resignation in connection with unauthorized
financial transactions caused serious strikes
and disorders, and his political and union career
ended in November 1964 with his expulsion from
the Socialist party.[2]

All that, however, came much later. In 1950
Olah was one of the heroes of the day. The
mobilization of his construction and woodworkers
when the police were so severely hampered in
their struggle against the unlawful occupation
of buildings, the obstruction of traffic and
communications, the interruption of railroad
movements was, if not decisive, at least of great
physical and even greater moral significance.

Why did the Soviet forces not intervene directly? We can only speculate on their motives, just
as we cannot be sure of any of the multiple

explanations suggested for the Soviet agreement
to the Austrian State Treaty of 1955. Despair
of or even contempt for the possibilities of decisive breakthroughs by the Austrian Communists
may have been a factor, or the fear of an open
clash with Western military forces in what looked
like a venture with exceedingly small prospects
of success. As Professor Bader puts it: "The
Soviet Union was simply not prepared to go the
limit."[3]

Did the Austrian Communists really intend to
go the limit and hope to acquire power? The vast
majority of observers at the time were convinced
that this was indeed the ultimate aim of the CP,
or at least this was what they asserted. The
union leaders stated it as well. Johann Böhm,
president of the OGB (Österreichischer Gewerk-
schaftsbund)—the trade union confederation—spoke
of a Communist putsch attempt. The Viennese
population, buying up what they could, clearly
feared the worst.

Still, it is difficult to believe that Karl
Altmann—whom I knew from university days as a
cool, calculating, and rather slow-moving man—
Ernst Fischer, a brilliant journalist and long-
time Social Democrat (until 1934); and some of
the other Communist leaders, really thought that
a party representing barely 5 percent of the
electorate could establish a viable government.
There are, in fact, reports of sharp disagreements at the time even within the CP leadership.
But if not the conquest of power, what then was
the Communist objective?

It would seem that the maximum they could hope
for was Soviet intervention that might reestablish their prestige as the allies of a superpower. Their minimum goal may have been the
conquest of some top positions in some of the
trade unions. As events turned out, they even
lost a good deal of the modest influence they

had had in the labor organizations. The Communist vice-president of the confederation, Gott-
lieb Fiala, was discharged as an employee of
the confederation and some eighty-five Communists were expelled from their respective trade
unions.

As to the Soviets, their main desire was to
prevent armed conflicts that might lead to
clashes between the Western occupation forces
and their own. That emerges pretty clearly
from a conversation between Friedl Fürnberg,
the Communist leader, and the Soviet authorities,
as reported by Ernst Fischer.

The fear of a putsch was thus exaggerated, but
its proclamation by Interior Minister Oscar Helmer and others may, at the time, have served its
purpose. What seems clear is the contempt in
which the Austrian party was held by its Soviet
protectors.

Notes

1. William Bader, *Austria between East and
West, 1945-1955* (Stanford, Calif.:   Stanford University Press, 1966), p. 161.

2. In March 1969, Olah was sentenced to one
year in jail for defraudation of trade union
funds. As the *Neue Zürcher Zeitung* (Zurich,
September 18, 1969) reported, Olah was in part
a victim of a power struggle, of his own "un-
orthodox" methods, and of his difficult personality. Olah claimed to have received support
from U.S. sources during 1950. He ascribed his
difficulties to the fact that the president of
the trade union confederation (OGB), Johann Böhm,
in February 1956 designated Olah as his future
successor, while others, especially Vice-President Maisel, felt they had a better claim. Olah
did indeed become president in 1959, after

Böhm's death.   Anton Benya took over as president of the OGB in 1963 when Olah became Minister of the Interior.

3.   Bader, *Austria*, p. 181.

WARE ADAMS

The Negative Veto–
A Breakthrough

Allied Control

The second agreement has already been written
about extensively. This paper is merely to see
whether I can fill any gaps in the discussion
from my experience at what is called the working
level, as State Department desk officer for Austrian affairs in the first half of 1945, and as
U.S. director of the political division of military government during the first two years of
the Allied Council, 1945-47. (I had been in our
embassy in London during the war, when the European Advisory Commission was established, but
had nothing to do with its work in 1944. I had
also been in Berlin during the Hitler era when
the Anschluss occurred, but had nothing whatever to do with that either, being then busy on
financial and economic reporting.) Since I am
no longer professionally active in either diplomacy or academic life, I speak not as historian
but only as one of many eyewitnesses whose impressions must wait to be summed up by the historians.

During the first half of 1945, the Central
European Division of the State Department (to
which I was assigned as desk officer for Aus-
trian affairs), handling matters concerning
Germany, Austria, and Czechoslovakia, served as
Washington base for communications with the
U.S. representative in the European Advisory
Commission and as liaison with the various parts

of the State Department and the military establishment in the planning for postwar arrangements and the interim periods of military government in the former battle areas.

Influences on policymaking converged from many
sides, all marked by the urgency and stress of
war and often requiring a decision by the President, who himself was sometimes hampered, as by
his contention with Churchill over whose occupation forces should be located in Southern Germany and whose in the North, where the ports
could facilitate supply by sea. Postwar planning necessitated the augmentation of regular
State Department staffs with experts from private and academic life, historians, geographers,
economists, bankers, and business men, and the
creation of a vast Civil Affairs Division in the
military establishment, fed by the special School
of Military Government at the University of Virginia.

The European Advisory Commission (EAC) had the
role of harmonizing the decisions, and the inde-
cisions, of three dissimilar national bureaucra-
cies. Its urgent priority was the surrender of
Germany and the zonal and control agreements for
it. The Instrument of Surrender, signed at Berlin finally on May 8, 1945, had a stark simplici-
ty. In the spirit of the controversial war cry
of "unconditional surrender," it said simply
that the Germans, in effect, surrendered to both
the Eastern and the Western Allies and would
follow orders received from them. But what if
the Allies should have differing, or even con-
flicting, orders to give? This is the question
that had to be faced in drafting the control
agreements. These provided that decisions concerning the country as a whole would be decided
by *unanimous* vote of the Allied Council, leaving other matters to be decided by each commander in and for his own zone.

After the tediously drawn-out EAC negotiations
on the agreements for Germany, the control machinery for Austria was hurriedly adapted from
that formulated for Germany—with suitable modi-
fications, including a provision envisaging further modification as the new Austrian state
emerged. It was with this, the first Control
Agreement, that the Allied Council was established in Vienna and began functioning. It soon
became evident in practice, in Austria as well
as in Germany, that this machinery was not very
workable. Quite apart from serious differences
of substance over which the council was often
deadlocked, it did not even work well for simple
matters. An amusing example was the council's
decision to have a joint Allied parade to cele-
brate the victory in Europe. When it came to
setting the date for it, each commander found
that his government at home had chosen a date
different from the other three for its own cele-
bration. How to avoid differentiating among the
four? The council exercised its supreme authority through a unanimous decision to have its parade on a date chosen by the Austrian authorities—a happy solution not always available. Was
this an augury for the future? By the end of
1945 we were all aware that the machinery was
not well designed for its purpose. We discussed
this in the quadripartite political division.
None of our four governments had sent us any
proposals for modification of the machinery.
We wondered whether we ourselves might develop
some improvements to submit to our respective
headquarters, although none of us as yet had
any specific reforms in mind to suggest.
    To try to develop some, I sat down quietly
over a weekend with the text of the existing
agreement beside my typewriter, rearranging or
rewriting its content while keeping as close as
possible to what seemed likely to be acceptable

to all four. I had the benefit of having followed the tedious negotiation through the EAC of
the first Austrian agreement, and of part of the
one for Germany, giving me a sense of certain
principles that were a must in order to be acceptable to all four, and of certain forms and
phrases that had seemed to be acceptable while
others had been rejected. The result was a tentative draft for a second control agreement. It
contained a new, as yet untested, provision in
Article 6 that laws of the Austrian government
would be proposed by that government to the Allied Council, and that after a specified time,
they would automatically become effective unless
disapproved by the council.

Although novel, this provision still complied
with two principles that had proven to be absolute prerequisites for four-power acceptance:
(1) Supreme authority must reside in the Allied
Council, and (2) council decisions must be
unanimous. The only novelty was that instead
of using its unanimous supreme authority to approve each law, the council would use it to
disapprove those deemed undesirable. If acceptable to the four powers, this would greatly sim-
plify procedures and enlarge the freedom and
authority of the Austrian government, while
still preserving those two principles already
proven vital to such acceptability.

Before offering my British, French, and Soviet
colleagues the draft, I took precautions against
having it rejected by my own headquarters. I
sent a copy to each of the fourteen directors of
divisions of the U.S. Element of the Allied
Council, and invited them all to a meeting in
the National Bank Building to discuss, and possibly to improve, the draft. All felt that if
it could be adopted it would improve operations
of the Allied Commission, and none had any
changes to suggest. I reported this to the

political adviser, and to my military superior,
the deputy high commissioner, General Gruenther,
for his information and that of General Clark,
and I requested permission to discuss and ex-
plore the draft with my British, French, and
Soviet colleagues.

At the next meeting of the political directorate, I gave copies to my colleagues, by way of
asking them whether they considered this suitable for our quadripartite division to recommend
to our respective headquarters, with such changes
or improvements as might occur to them meanwhile.
While they looked it over, the British member
(Nicholls) remarked enthusiastically that it was
"ingenious." The French and Soviet directors
said they would study it. It encouraged me that
they had no adverse comment to make at that
point. I invited them all, when they had had a
chance to study it, to meet to discuss it, and
possibly to amend or improve it, to make it a
joint draft of our quadripartite division to
recommend to our respective superiors. I said
I had not yet suggested it to Washington, pre-
ferring first to know how each of them felt
about it.

Two or three weeks later my British colleague
telephoned me to say he had informally discussed
the draft with London, where they liked it so
much they had authorized a British proposal to
the secretariat that it be considered formally
by the Allied Council, thus bringing it before
all four governments.

From then on, the discussions in the Allied
Council and in the council's Executive Committee are on the record. Records of divisional
meetings below that level were not kept by the
secretariat, but only by each element for its
own purposes. When I tried to research my records in 1969, the files could not be found by
either the embassy or the historian of the State

Department, leaving only memory for an account
I was trying to write.

In after years much American comment assumed
that Article 6 must somehow have slipped by the
Soviet authorities without much notice. But
this is not the case. For about six months before its signature, there was both formal and
informal discussion of the proposed agreement,
especially Article 6, at all levels. After one
Executive Committee meeting, the Soviet deputy
high commissioner, General Zheltov, had a private
meeting with the U.S. deputy high commissioner
and me, exploring from all sides the implications
and probable out-working of Article 6. General
Zheltov was a highly intelligent man of acute
perception and carried out admirably the negotiator's role of exploring not only the substance
under negotiation but also the probable purposes
of the other negotiators. At one point he turned
to me smiling, pointed to my briefcase, and
asked: "Have you any reserves in there?" We had
none. His attitude was not one of either acceptance or rejection, but rather of exploring the
intricacies of an interesting puzzle, to see
whether there might be a better way. I have been
told by Danish historian Peter Sørensen that General Zheltov also had a similar exploratory talk
with his British opposite number, General Winter-
ton.[1]

On another occasion, a meeting of the political
directorate was attended by a substitute for the
Soviet director, in the person of a general never
seen before or after, who gave the appearance of
a specialist, either legal or political (possibly on a mission from Moscow?). He presented a
lengthy argument about constitutional difficulties inherent in Article 6, leaving a large shadow of doubt about Soviet acceptance.

Since the control agreement was itself a sort
of basic constitution governing the Allied Council

and the Allied Commission, it concerned the work
of all of its divisions, and no doubt it was discussed in most of them.   One that was especially
interested, and concerned, was the legal division.   I have an impression from its then director, Col. Eberhardt Deutsch (later honorary consul of Austria in New Orleans) that much good
was done there towards clarifying in Soviet minds
the distinction between ordinary laws and constitutional laws, thus removing a likely obstacle
to Soviet agreement.[2]

In any case, Article 6, which originally was
drafted to include all laws, was amended to cover
"laws, other than constitutional laws," which
seemed to make it more acceptable to the Soviet
element.   Had they feared a constitutional change
towards renewed Anschluss?   I don't know.   In any
case the change did not disturb us.   The State Department had great respect for Prof. Hans Kelsen's
constitutional law, and the spirit at least of the
constitution of 1920-29 had already been adopted
by the Renner government with Soviet approval, and
continued to prevail despite nervous Soviet edgi-
ness about constitutional law questions.

The Control Agreement, once signed, worked
well, and continued to do so as far as I know,
until the end.   There were throughout, of course,
great differences among the Allies, notably on
German assets.   But these would have been there
with or without the second Control Agreement—and
much worse without it.   The agreement remained
intact and respected.   I feel impelled to remind
my American friends of this when they say the
Russians do not keep agreements.   In my own limited experience, I found them to be rather le-
galistic instead.

They were not alone in nervous reticence.
They were the first to stand up in the Allied
Council and announce readiness to sign.   The
last to do so, I must confess, was the U.S.

While we were awaiting the green light to sign
the agreement, Washington sent us a telegram
postponing it, and expressing "grave misgivings" about Article 6.[3] It was only later that
American comment ran in terms of "The Miracle
of Austria—a Diplomatic Success Story."

When the new agreement was finally signed,
the political division of the Allied Commission
had a festive dinner, hosted by our French director, M. Padovani, at which all four of us
exchanged autographed, embossed copies of "our"
agreement. (Mine seems to have gotten lost with
the files of the office.)

In the following year there were many policy
disputes, but only once did my Soviet colleague
say to me sadly that "no one ever thought the
agreement would turn out this way." What he
really meant, I think, was that no one ever
thought the U.S. would ever use its veto power
that way—not that the control machinery was badly designed—for the result would have been the
same under the first agreement, since both required unanimity for any positive action. The
occasion was a slurring jingle published by an
Austrian newspaper that mocked the treatment of
labor unions in the Soviet Union. The Soviet
member wanted the Allied Commission to reprimand
the paper for demeaning one of the four powers.
The American member vetoed his proposal, in line
with our principle of freedom of the press. It
was simply incomprehensible to the Russians that
the Americans would condone an insult to the
dignity of one of the occupying powers, and they
took it as an anti-Soviet action on our part,
embittering relations in the council. I pri-
vately regretted having to use the new agreement
for this petty purpose, and agreed with President Renner's advice to his countrymen against
needlessly twisting the tail of the Russian bear
in occupation of the country.

During the first two years of the Allied Commission I never once heard the word *neutrality*.
But I remember well that before anyone could decide whether the second agreement was desirable
or not, he had to consider in what directions
Austria might go if free to do so on its own.
Most Americans had no doubts about this. More
fundamental than a required or declared neutrality would be the basic inner nature and personality of Austria, something that could not be put
into a single word or phrase, but might have a
broader description something like this, if I may
wander on my own—

*In itself, an independent Austria poses no danger
or threat to anybody. The world recognizes this.
At the same time, Austria is at the heart of Europe, geographically, culturally, and intellec-
tually, with a long and varied history rich in
learning experience, often turbulent and bitter-
ly painful, but educational, resulting in a matu-
rity of understanding, of itself and of others,
and thus able to help others understand each
other.*

Notes

1.   See Peter Sørensen, *Østrigs genomprettlese
efter 2. verdenskrig* (Århus, Denmark: Århus
Universitet, 1968).

2.   See ibid., for an annexed letter of November
21, 1967, from Dr. Albert Loewy of Vienna, who
was a captain in the legal division at the time,
discussing Soviet views of constitutional law
in Austria.

3.   Secret telegram no. 543, June 11, 1946, in
U.S. Department of State, *Foreign Relations of
the U.S., 1946, Austria* (Washington, D.C.:
Government Printing Office, 1968), 5:348-49.

WILLIAM B. BADER

Austria, The United States, and the Path to Neutrality

For a country that is as small as the state of
Georgia and holds a population slightly less
than the city of Los Angeles, it is remarkable
just how many Austrians have become serious and
recognized participants in American political
life and culture. Whatever the state of the
average American's knowledge of Austria and Austrian history, there is no doubt that the array
of Austrians who have come to live and work
amongst us have made a deep and enduring impression on American life. Such names as Felix
Frankfurter, Otto Preminger, Rudolf Bing, Fritz
Kreisler, Paul Muni, Hattie Carnegie, and Billy
Wilder represent only the most prominent van-
guard of an impressive "invasion."

Of the major waves of Austrian emigration that
came to the United States, none was more impressive than that of the 1930s—drawn largely from
Social Democrats, Socialists, and Laborists,
many of them driven to the United States by Dollfuss after 1934. Through the time of Dollfuss
to that of Hitler, Austria would send this country many of its "best and brightest"; men and
women who could have expected nothing at home
but harassment, contempt, or concentration camps.
There were philosophers, artists, artisans, and
politicians: a contingent as rich in culture,
experience, and potential as any that has
reached this country.

I mention this exodus and odyssey because it
is my very strong impression that during the war

years the Austrian émigré community played little to no role in the formation of American policy with regard to Austria. I grant that there were a number of Austrian newspapers in this country as well as various Austrian community and action groups that worked for the reestablishment of a free Austria. While one might like to believe that the Austrian émigré community had access to the White House and the State Department, this, as far as I can determine, was not the case. It is true that Otto von Habsburg almost hopelessly complicated the Austrian situation by advocating within the U.S. not only a return to the monarchy but an Austrian battalion in the American army. The fact is, however, that the Austrians never succeeded in either setting up a government in exile or organizing the kind of pressure and information groups that could influence the outcome of Allied discussions and negotiations over the future of Austria.

In my own view, this distance between the Austrian exile community and the U.S. government machinery contributed significantly to the strong sense of abstraction and political naiveté of the Americans who in 1943 to 1945 worried—however fleetingly—about Austria's future. And that naiveté was never more dramatically displayed than during the period when the European Advisory Commission served as the forum for Allied discussion and debate on the occupation of Europe.

It should be noted that the European Advisory Commission (EAC), which evolved from the political military commission that Stalin had pressured his allies into establishing in September of 1943, was designed to handle not only our negotiations with defeated enemies but all political matters that the Big Three chose to refer to it.

To all of us who have puzzled over the machinations of the EAC with regard to the establishment of a control authority for Austria, it has become

clear over time that part of the reason for
scholarly confusion is that the EAC was viewed
from Washington in terms of one major concern—a
concern, as George Kennan put it, "lest the new
body should at some point and by some mischance
actually do something."[1] In my view, the cha-
otic manner in which the U.S. government finally
arrived at a policy on the Austrian occupation
illustrates vividly the consequences of what
must be seen historically as a profound case of
bureaucratic indifference and contradiction.
The State Department, the Joint Chiefs of Staff,
and the White House all conspired to pursue
their own policies and in the process rendered
the EAC a confusing and basically unworkable commission. As John Winant himself concluded:
"I do not think that any conference or commission created by governments for a serious purpose has less support from the governments creating it than the European Advisory Commission."[2]

   If we try to sort out the American priorities
and politics of 1943-45 regarding Austria, we
confront such a bewildering array of contradictory policies and positions that even the most
artful historian can make little sense of them.
Consider the statement, for example, of Robert
Murphy, the political advisor on the staff of
General Eisenhower, that it: "Could have been
a comparatively simple matter for the U.S. Third
Army to have penetrated deeply into Czechoslovakia and to have taken Prague. In the absence of
a directive, however, General Eisenhower's
strategy laid emphasis on facilitating the occupation of Southern Germany and Western Austria, thus paving the way for the longer term
occupation."[3] This appraisal was sent to the
Secretary of State by Murphy in early May of
1945, just at a time that the White House was
steadfastly resisting any U.S. postwar presence
in southern Germany and Austria.

It remains uncertain why President Roosevelt
was so insistent that U.S. forces should occupy
the northwestern parts of Germany, while Austria
and the Balkans would be exclusive Soviet and
British responsibility. But insistent he was;
and when confronted by John Winant's determined
effort to obtain presidential approval of tri-
partite occupation in Austria, he cabled Churchill with the emphatic message: "France, Austria
and the Balkans will not be included in the American zone of responsibility."[4] As late as July 15,
1944, Winant was receiving the instructions that,
"in conformity with the President's instructions
to you, to accept the protocol provided that it
is expressly understood that only a token occupation force for Austria will be provided by the
United States."[5]

As for the Department of State and any sense
developing there of long-term responsibility in
southern Europe, the president left no doubt where
he stood on the question of American troops of occupation there:

*In view of my clearly stated inability to police
the south and southwestern areas now occupied by
the Germans, I really think it is necessary that
General Eisenhower shall even now make such plans
as are practical to use American forces of occupation in northwestern Europe during the occupation
period. Such plans as it is practicable for
Eisenhower to prepare in advance would help to
meet the contingency of your not being able to
provide forces of occupation in all of the surrendered and liberated areas not occupied by the
Soviets and of my inability to police the southern
areas—France, Italy, etc.*[6]

By the end of August then, the United States had
come only so far as to approve a plan whereby Austria would be divided into two zones to be occupied

respectively by the armed forces of the Soviet
Union and of the United Kingdom. Only Vienna was
seen as a combined zone to be occupied by the
forces of the three powers.

Perhaps prompted by the developments in Bulgaria and Romania, where it was becoming start-
lingly clear that the ability to influence grew
directly out of military power on the ground,
Winant pressed on for greater U.S. participation
in the occupation and management of Austria. In
December of 1944, Winant made one more effort,
ending his argument to Roosevelt by cable with a
strong and unequivocal statement that:

*In view of our leading position in the conduct
of the war and the settlement of the peace, and
in view of Austria's key position in Central
Europe, our refusal to take a zone of occupation
may be interpreted as a sign that we are willing
to leave this area to the free play of Soviet
and British interests....I have great doubts as
to the ultimate wisdom of leaving British interests pitted against Russian interest in Austria....Twice in 25 years we have been drawn into world war because of disturbances in European areas far distant from us and in which we
have exercised little influence. In neither instance did we control the events which ultimately involved us in war.*[7]

Time—and the press of political events and realities—brought Roosevelt gradually and grudg-
ingly to Winant's position. Churchill had succeeded in September at Quebec in persuading, if
not dragooning, the president into believing
that the United States should accept the southern part of Germany as its area of occupation.
Once the breakthrough with respect to southern
Germany had been made, it was now not all that
difficult to convince Roosevelt of the need for

an Austrian zone contiguous to the American area
in Germany. Although there was much pulling and
hauling with respect to the exact zones of occupation and the time of Allied occupation of Austria, the Austrian control council agreement was
finally signed on July 9, 1945, and two weeks
later, Soviet troops were withdrawn to their zone.
On July 28, the Allied Commission in Vienna began
to function. The reluctant Americans had arrived.
If Roosevelt had known how long they would remain
there, he might very well have been able to resist the blandishments of Winant.

However difficult it may have been to convince
Americans to participate in the occupation of
Austria, that effort can hardly be compared to
the prolonged struggle to convince the Russians
to leave. Much has been written about the long
Austrian march to freedom. And that long march
need not be retold here. Let me offer a few observations, however, on the continuing enigma of
the Soviet withdrawal from Austria.

After ten years of occupation and frustration,
Austria in 1955 was suddenly cast into the free
world—now neutralized and virtually demilitarized
because of the stringent military clauses in the
treaty, but free. Obviously a bit nonplussed by
the sudden turn of events, the United States Senate Committee on Foreign Relations noted in its
report of the draft treaty: "In the space of
seven weeks, between the Soviet invitation and
the signing, every obstacle thrown up during the
previous seven years was withdrawn or compromised by the Soviet Union and a treaty acceptable
to the Western Powers and Austria was signed."[8]

It is now over twenty-five years since V. M.
Molotov signed the Austrian State Treaty for the
Soviet Union, an event that marked the first—and
thus far the *only*—time the Soviet Union has con-
sented to a major readjustment of the rough line
of demarcation established in Europe by World

War II. Thus, not only was the event unprece-
dented, but the precipitous, almost bizzare,
manner in which it was carried out has prompted
continuing speculation on the lingering enigma
of the Soviet withdrawal.

The most prevalent view of the Soviet move em-
phasizes the net gains for the West accruing from
the Soviet decision, or uses the eventual success
of the negotiations as an example of what can
happen if we persist in negotiating with the Soviets. This general satisfaction of the West
with the 1955 solution to the "Austrian problem"
was most exuberantly expressed by Secretary of
State John Foster Dulles in his report to the
American people on May 17, 1955, after his return
from Vienna. Dulles recalled the sense of frustration that had marked the long struggle to
achieve an Austrian treaty, a struggle that had
gone on without success throughout 379 separate
meetings by the end of 1954. Then, as he put it:

*All of a sudden, a few weeks ago, out of the
blue, came this announcement that the Russians
were willing to take their troops out of Austria.
I don't think anyone yet knows fully the significance—the full significance—of that. It is just
one of those breaks that come if you keep on
steadily, steadily, keeping the pressure on. And
all of a sudden you get a break—and this break
came—*

*This is the first time a segment of the Red
Army will have turned around and started to go
back. Now that is going to have a tremendous
impact in the other countries where the Red Armies are in occupation. It is going to create
a desire—a mounting desire—on the part of those
people to get the same freedom from that type
of occupation that the Austrians have got....*

*Why they are doing it, we are not quite sure.
Except that we can be quite certain the policies*

of strength and firmness that we are adopting
in partnership with the other free countries
of Europe, are beginning to pay off. And the
people of Austria are the first to say—and all
of them did say to me—this is the first dividend
from the creation of Western European unity and
the bringing of Germany into NATO.[9]

Although John Foster Dulles saw the Soviet decision to leave Austria as "just one of those
breaks that come if you keep on steadily, steadily, keeping the pressure on," he was forced to
concede personally to President Eisenhower that
"the cause of this change of policy can only be
conjectured."[10]

What follows is also conjecture, but conjecture formed against a backdrop of what we now
know about the course of those events inside and
outside Austria that shaped, and possibly also
explain, the Soviet decision.

As the year 1955 began, the Soviet Union could
hardly have been pleased with the events of the
preceding twelve months. The military advantage
they had attained in 1953 by exploding a usable
hydrogen weapon (the United States had tested an
admittedly undeliverable hydrogen device some
months before) had been lost with the successful testing of a U.S. hydrogen bomb in early
1954. On the economic front, the Soviet Union
was faced with a serious grain crisis at a moment when Malenkov's emphasis on the consumer
economy was detracting from military expendi-
tures. Perhaps even more adverse to Soviet interests than a momentary imbalance of military
power and a faltering economy was Moscow's lack
of success in preventing the military integration of West Germany into the Western Alliance.
Molotov's insistence at the Berlin conference
that there would be no Austrian settlement until a solution of the German problem acceptable

to Moscow had been worked out was just one more
way of raising the price for bringing West Germany into the Western Alliance.

One of the more interesting sidelights of this
intensive and ultimately unsuccessful campaign
was that the Soviets had made little use of its
hostage, eastern Austria, in attempting to frus-
trate the entry of West Germany into the Western
Alliance. Molotov's speech on February 8 came
far too late to have any real effect on the West
German decision. Had the Soviets made the offer
of exchanging Austrian neutralization or reunification in, say, the spring of 1954 and held out
the possibility of a similar deal in Germany,
the gesture could have been very helpful in keeping West Germany out of the North Atlantic Treaty
Organization (NATO). Why the Soviet Union waited
so long to bring forth the Austrian offer—and
then finally did so for reasons that seem only
partially related to Germany—remains somewhat of
a mystery. The best explanation probably lies
in the nature of the power struggle that was then
going on within the Kremlin.

In the meantime, while the Warsaw Pact consolidated security arrangements within Eastern Europe,
the Soviet Union sought to lessen Western military pressures by initiating a campaign against
military alliances and for disarmament and neutralism. The pilgrimage to Belgrade to make
peace with Tito, the public relations junkets of
Khrushchev and Bulganin, Soviet enthusiasm for
the 1955 Bandung Conference of Afro-Asians, the
disarmament proposals of May 10, 1955, the invitation to Adenauer to visit Moscow, the offer to
conclude a peace treaty with Japan—these were all
part of the same diplomatic offensive. But most
of all, Khrushchev wanted a "summit" meeting.
And here the Austrian hostage played a major role.

Even after the meeting was arranged, Secretary
Dulles had nothing but the gravest misgivings.

In a confidential memorandum to the president,
he listed among the "Soviet goals at Geneva":
"An appearance that the West concede the Soviet
rulers a moral and social equality which will
help the Soviets maintain their satellite rule
by disheartening potential resistance, *and help
increase neutralism by spreading the impression
that only power rivalries, and not basic principles, create present tensions.*"[11]

As to the possibility of preventing Soviet
success in achieving these goals, Dulles was
gloomy. On the matter of achieving "moral and
social equality," Dulles wrote: "The Soviets
will probably make considerable gains in this
respect. These gains can be minimized by the
President avoiding social meetings where he will
be photographed with Bulganin, Khrushchev, etc.,
and by maintaining an austere countenance on occasions where photographing together is inevitable."[12]

In letting Austria go, Khrushchev probably
reasoned that since the country could not be
peacefully assimilated into the "Socialist camp,"
signing the State Treaty would not be too expensive, for the following reasons.

1. By 1955, the strategic and political neces-
    sity for maintaining a forward and insulat-
    ing zone in Austria had largely disappeared.
    Until 1948 Austria could have been con-
    sidered a military and political staging
    area for probes against Western Europe.
    With the military unification and political
    pacification of Western Europe, Eastern Aus-
    tria had become an exposed position for the
    Soviet Union. The Czechoslovakia border
    provided a more defensible military line.
    Then too, Khrushchev probably thought that
    his Eastern European political house was in
    order by 1955, and that an insulating zone

such as Stalin had used in 1949-50 was un-
necessary. (A year later he would not have
been so sure.) Moreover, until 1955, the
continuance of the Austrian occupation had
given the Soviets the treaty right to keep
troops in Romania and Hungary. The Warsaw
Pact now gave the Soviets the same rights,
this time in Czechoslovakia as well.

2. The military and political restrictions imposed on Austria by the treaty are such that
not only is Anschluss with Germany forbidden,
but Austria is now virtually a military vacuum in the center of Europe. Because Czechoslovakia and Hungary can fortify their Austrian borders and West Germany and Italy cannot
(this is not a treaty provision but simply a
political reality), Austria forms a conveni-
ent gateway to attack on Western Europe.

3. With the neutralization of Austria, the lines
of communication and supply between two of
the most important NATO countries—West Germany and Italy—must now pass through France
(the Austrian prohibition of military over-
flights during the 1958 Lebanon crisis and
the 1973 Middle East war are examples of the
problems created for the West by Austria's
strategic position). The difficulties of
moving men and supplies from the Elbe to
Verona illustrate the logistic problems
caused by the neutralization of Austria.

4. Austria had become by 1955 an economic liability, thereby removing one of the major
reasons for continued Soviet occupation.
Austrian oil was no longer a useful commodi-
ty for the Soviets, who by this time had
enough domestic oil to threaten the world
markets of the West. Moreover, the Soviet-
controlled industries in Austria had been
on the verge of bankruptcy for a number of

years, utterly unable to compete on the Austrian market (the massive rehabilitation job necessary after 1955 is evidence of this).

5. For the Soviets there was no particular ideological problem involved in the release of Austria. The Austrians, even in the Soviet zone, had never embraced Communist dogma; consequently, they remained, in Soviet eyes, ideological infidels—a condition certainly more acceptable to the Soviets than if the Austrians had first embraced and then attempted to renounce communism.

In 1956, the Hungarians were to learn how the Soviets deal with converts who consider apostasy. Furthermore, as long as the Soviet Union had control of an area where political dissent was openly expressed, and was apparently tolerated by the Soviets, there was always the possibility that this pocket of discontent could begin to affect the rest of Eastern Europe.

Often cited as a powerful justification for Khrushchev's action has been a Soviet long-term calculation that the Austrian settlement would serve as a model—an inducement for some to accept demilitarization, and pointing up for others the advantages of staying out of military alliances.

John Foster Dulles, for one, was not optimistic about the United States's chance of countering the so-called Geneva line. In an assessment of the Geneva meeting written for President Eisenhower in August 1955, Dulles wrote:

Geneva has certainly created problems for the free nations. For eight years they have been held together largely by a cement compounded of fear and a sense of moral superiority. Now the fear is diminished and the moral demarcation is somewhat blurred. There is some bewilderment among leaders and peoples of the free nations as to what happened, and as to how to adjust to the new situation.[13]

Whether the Austrian solution seriously weakened the Western "cement compounded of fear and a sense of moral superiority" is doubtful at best. Secretary Dulles despised ambiguity, and Austria was ushered into an ambiguous condition in 1955. But there is little evidence that Austria became a model for nations with neutral "tendencies."

In closing, I submit a personal observation as to why the Soviet occupation of Austria did not "take." Throughout the occupation, there seemed to be something innately hostile in the makeup of the slightly cynical, traditionally negative, often hypercivilized Austrian toward the tough, ideologically minded Soviet. If the long years of Socialist-Conservative warfare and Nazi occupation had had any effect on the individual Austrian, they had convinced him that ideological excesses are foolish and dangerous. The two stereotypes—the herculean Ivan and the ultra-cynical Herr Karl in most Austrians—mixed badly. This "mixture" surely contributed to what became a free and independent Austria. And it was not a small contribution.

Notes

1. Quoted in John Lewis Gaddis, *The United States and the Origins of the Cold War, 1941-1947* (New York: Columbia University Press, 1972), p. 47.

2. Ibid., p. 49.

3. Political Address of Robert Murphy to the Secretary of State, May 11, 1945, *Foreign*

Relations of the United States, 1945 (Washington, D.C.: Government Printing Office, 1968), 4:451. (This title is hereafter cited as *FRUS*.)

4. President Roosevelt to Prime Minister Churchill, May 27, 1944, *FRUS, 1944*, 1:223.

5. *FRUS, 1944*, 1:451.

6. President Roosevelt to Prime Minister Churchill, June 2, 1944, *FRUS, 1944*, 1:232.

7. *FRUS, 1944*, 1:477.

8. "U.S. Senate Committee on Foreign Relations Report," June 15, 1955, *American Foreign Policy, 1950–1955* (Washington, D.C.: Government Printing Office, 1955), 1:685.

9. "An Historic Week—Report to the President," U.S. Department of State, pp. 6-8.

10. *American Foreign Policy, 1950-1955*, 1:679.

11. "Dulles Papers—Category IX," August 15, 1955, Conference Dossiers, Special Subjects, December 1954-55.

12. "Estimate of the Prospect of the Soviet Union Achieving Its Goals" (n.d.), ibid.

13. From a memorandum proposed by Dulles for the president and then sent to United States chiefs of mission for background information, August 15, 1955, ibid.

WILLIAM A. STEARMAN

An Analysis of Soviet
Objectives in Austria

The Advantages of the Occupation

From the standpoint of avowed Soviet expansionist goals, the continued occupation of Austria
always had appeared to be advantageous to the
Soviet Union. Western observers of the Austrian scene offered a number of reasons why the
Soviets remained in Austria but saw few, if
any, reasons why the Soviet Union should ever
withdraw its troops from Austrian soil.

Generally considered among the most important
factors was the Soviet right to station lines
of communication troops in Hungary and Rumania
that derived from the Soviet occupation of eastern Austria. The presence of Soviet troops in
these countries ensured the installation of Communist regimes and undoubtedly contributed to
political pressure on Czechoslovakia, which was
communized without Soviet troops.[1] As was later
demonstrated, however, the withdrawal of Soviet
troops from Austria did not have to result in
the evacuation of Hungary and Rumania. Nonetheless, the importance the Soviets attached to
controlling Austria's borders with Hungary and
Czechoslovakia was clearly demonstrated in 1945
during Allied negotiations.

This article first appeared as chapter eight
in Stearman, *The Soviet Union and the Occupation
of Austria* (Vienna, Bonn, Zurich: Siegler & Co.,
1962).

The Soviets certainly derived important economic advantages from the occupation. Not only were
they able to exploit Austria's oilfields and the
USIA (Administration of Soviet Property in Austria) enterprises, but they were able, in Austria,
to create a crack in the Iron Curtain through
which they could, through devious channels, obtain raw materials and manufactured products that
the West had, for strategic reasons, embargoed
for sale to the Soviet orbit.[2] This same crack
was also utilized for what amounted to wholesale
smuggling of goods into and through Austria.

Occupied Austria not only provided a significant economic link with the West, but also fulfilled a similar political function. Among other
things, Soviet control of part of Vienna enabled
international Communist-front organizations to
set up headquarters and to organize conferences
and demonstrations in a Western, non-Communist
European capital. Initially, the Soviets had
hopes of communizing Austria; however, the decisive Communist electoral defeats in 1945 and 1949
and the abortive general-strike attempt in 1950
must have convinced them that communism was a
hopeless cause in Austria, with or without direct
Soviet support.

Psychological, political, and military inhibi-
tions undoubtedly also influenced the Soviet decision to remain in Austria. Not since the 1945
demarcation-line adjustments in Austria and the
1946 evacuation of Iran had Soviet troops been
withdrawn from World War II points of farthest
advance. As the cold war progressed and fronts
stiffened and froze, the Kremlin might well have
feared psychological and political consequences
of any shrinking of their *Machtbereich* (sphere
of influence). Soviet generals were also probably reluctant to give up their bases in eastern
Austria even though the flat terrain they held
could be quickly reoccupied from Hungary in an
all-out war.

Despite all those factors, the Soviet zone of
Austria was the only area held by Soviet troops
after 1946—except for isolated bases—that was
not brought under Communist control. This was,
of course, theoretically just as possible in
Austria as in Germany and would have led to the
same result, the complete partitioning of the
country; however, as Foreign Minister Gruber
pointed out in a 1952 speech: "...the few advantages that such a partition would bring the
East could not outweigh great disadvantages in
economic, military, and political respects, not
to speak of the reaction that such an unheard-
of provocation would evoke in world opinion,
which must quickly lead to the mobilization of
the whole free world."[3]

The economic disadvantages referred to by
Gruber would have been the severance of east
Austrian industries from their principal internal sources of such important resources as steel,
iron ore, aluminum, several vital minerals, industrial chemicals, fertilizer, and electricity,
to name only a few.[4] In short, a partitioned
east Austria separated from important raw material sources in the country would have been more
of an economic liability than an asset to the
Soviets.

The military disadvantages of partition to the
Soviets would have been the building up of an
Austrian army in western Austria that would have
augmented U.S., British, and French forces in
the country.

Most of the political drawbacks of a split
Austria are obvious. In the first place, the
freely elected central government of the country would, in all probability, have remained in
Vienna and would have continued to represent
most of the country. The formal establishment
of an east Austrian government on the German
pattern would have been difficult, if for no

other reason than a lack of adequate personnel.
The Soviet zone contained only 27 percent—mostly
anti-Communist—of Austria's 7,000,000 inhabitants
(35 percent if the Soviet sector of Vienna is included); Vienna, however, with its split sectors
and quadripartitely controlled center, would have
been far more difficult to divide than was Berlin, and armed Soviet occupation of the Western
or international sectors would not only have constituted a casus belli but, after 1949, also an
attack against NATO.

Another factor militating against a Soviet partitioning of Austria was the prospect of losing
a degree of control over western Austria—particularly in such matters as disarmament—by withdrawing from the Allied agreements that made it
possible for the Soviet element to exercise a
veto power in certain fields affecting the whole
country.[5]

Probably militating against both the partitioning of Austria and the ending of the occupation
was the importance of Austria as a bargaining
factor. Chess-playing Russians might well have
long regarded the withdrawal of Soviet troops
from Austria as a political gambit whereby the
"pawn," the Soviet zone of Austria, could be
sacrificed in order ultimately to place the Western "king" in check.[6]

Why the Occupation of Austria Ended

During the April 1955 Austro-Soviet negotiations, Soviet Premier Bulganin reportedly told
the Austrians, "we are not agreeing to an Austrian state treaty out of pity for Austria."[7] If
unmoved by pity, the Kremlin was also hardly
motivated by a sudden Austrian decision to become neutral. For years, the leaders of both
government parties had advocated a policy of
neutrality and nonalliance with military blocks,

and the Soviets had shown little if any interest.[8] Moreover, the Russians didn't sign the
State Treaty because they had won better terms.
On the contrary, they could have had a far more
favorable treaty in past years. What then did
the Soviet leaders think they would gain by
granting Austria her freedom?

One not easily recognizable clue may be found
in Molotov's speech of February 8, 1955, in which
he called for the signing of the Austrian treaty
and stated that, "in case the Paris Agreements
were ratified, which would pave the way for a
revival of militarism in West Germany, there
would arise a great danger of Anschluss and
therefore a great danger to Austria's independence."[9] From this and other similar statements
in the Molotov speech, it might therefore be
deduced that the signing of the State Treaty
was somehow regarded by the Soviets as a blow
against the Paris Agreements, which were designed to bolster Western Europe's defense a-
gainst the Soviet bloc and specifically to bring
about West Germany's participation in this defense. The reasons why the Soviets would want
to wreck such plans were obvious. But if the
Soviets actually did believe that by signing the
Austrian Treaty they would weaken Western Europe's defense and would affect West Germany's
contributions to this defense, on what did they
base their calculations?

The Paris Agreements were signed between October 19 and 23, 1954.[10] The Soviet Union immediately reacted with an intense propaganda and
diplomatic campaign, and on November 13 invited
the United States and the European countries to
a "European Security Conference" to be held in
Moscow to discuss the Paris Agreements. At this
conference, which ended on December 2, 1954, and
which was attended only by Soviet bloc countries,
it was decided to form a formal Communist

counterpart to NATO in case the Paris Agreements
were ratified.[11] Augmenting this warning, the
Soviets, eleven days later, told the Austrians
that "aggressive North Atlantic Bloc" activities
were jeopardizing the country's unity and added
to this veiled threat of partition the more ex-
plicit warning that ratification of the Paris
Agreement would end Austria's chances for a treaty.[12]

Apparently realizing that this blackmail would
not work, the line was completely reversed in
Molotov's February 8, 1955, speech, which implied
that the ratification of the Paris Agreements
would necessitate a state treaty in order to protect Austria's independence from West Germany.[13]
That the Soviets did not really consider ratification a hindrance to concluding the State Treaty
was proven by the simple fact that the final ratification of the Paris Agreements on May 5, 1955,
in no way affected the treaty negotiations then
in progress in Vienna. However, on May 14, 1955,
the day before the Austrian treaty was signed,
the Soviet Union and her European satellites
agreed in Warsaw to the (in fact, pro forma)
formation of an Eastern counterpart of NATO with
a unified command—headed by Soviet Marshal (and
first Soviet high commissioner in Austria) I. S.
Koniev—and an agreement that the troop distribu-
tion within the member states would be "carried
out in agreement between these states."[14] This,
in effect, provided the Soviets with a legal
pretext for the continued stationing of troops
in Hungary and Rumania after the Austrian treaty
had cancelled the legal right to maintain lines
of communications forces in these countries, as
stipulated in their peace treaties.[15]

It appears almost certain that the Soviet desire to conclude a state treaty was not primarily aimed at preventing the ratification of the
Paris Agreements. When the first Soviet treaty

feelers were made in February and March, ratification was not assured, but when the final Austro-
Soviet agreements were concluded in April, ratification, having been approved by the parliaments
of the participating states, was a certainty. If
the Soviets were, in fact, primarily using the
Austrian treaty as a weapon against the Paris
Agreements, the intention must have been to make
the best of a fait accompli and to hinder the implementation of these agreements.

The Austrian Treaty and Western Defense

Perhaps the most significant aspect of Ilyi-
shev's surprise Allied Council attack of December 21, 1954, against the stationing of U.S.
troops in the French zone was the accusation
that these troops were manning supply and communication lines between West Germany and Italy.
Although obscured in propaganda, one valid advantage of a neutral Austria to the Soviets was
indicated in this accusation. When the last
Western troops left Austria, there remained a
neutral wedge 530 miles (850 km) long (from
Bratislava to Geneva) that split Italy from West
Germany—less than six months after they had been
joined together for defense purposes in the
"Western European Union"—and which therefore
split NATO and the whole Western defense in two.
What the Paris Agreements had joined together,
the State Treaty, at least partly, put asunder.
The Soviets made no attempts to disguise this
goal. On April 16, 1955, Pravda characterized
the Austro-Soviet agreement on the treaty as "a
blow against the policy of forming military
blocks in Europe."[16]
There were clear indications that Western
military experts and those responsible for the
defense of Western Europe were concerned about
the problems raised by Austria's neutrality.[17]

There were reports that Italy now felt isolated
and that Switzerland felt threatened by what was
regarded as a newly formed military vacuum on
her eastern border.[18] The most detailed and outspoken criticism of the military situation created by Austria's neutrality was an article in
the *Neue Zürcher Zeitung* of August 23, 1955,
which pointed out the strategic disadvantages to
the NATO powers caused by the loss of positions
in western Austria and the splitting of the Western defense front, and which drew attention to
the danger to Switzerland of the "military vacuum" in Austria: "The Sargans Fortress [on Switzerland's eastern border] had become a fortress
on the Russian border," as the paper expressed
it. The *Neue Zürcher Zeitung* further maintained
that any disadvantages to the Soviets entailed
in withdrawing to Hungary were canceled out by
the ease with which Soviet troops could reoccupy
the flat, easily accessible, and difficult-to-
defend area they had evacuated.

In reply to this article, the Vienna daily
Neues Österreich of September 1, 1955, pointed
out that present trends indicated that the great
powers would pursue their policies "with other
means"; that the Soviets wouldn't have given up
their Austrian position if they had had the intention to push the Iron Curtain further west;
that in the event of war the plains of northern
and central Germany would be more suitable for
a mass attack than the Austrian alpine regions;
that in the event of a violation of Austrian
neutrality, NATO troops in southern Germany and
northern Italy would be no farther from Austria
than Soviet troops in Hungary; and that it was
better for Switzerland that Austria be neutral
than to continue as a "permanent battlefield in
the cold war."

Regardless of the remoteness of war or direct military threats to Austria, a rough

comparison of Austria's military strength with
that of her eastern Communist neighbors must
have been sobering to the most confirmed opti-
mist. Nearly a year after the signing of the
State Treaty, Austrian armed forces numbered
little over 6,000 men, a large part of whom
were in the early stages of training; furthermore, it was estimated that on the second anniversary of her freedom, Austria would still have
only 30,000 troops under arms, at which time
Soviet and national armies in Hungary and Czechoslovakia would, according to Austrian estimates,
outnumber Austrian forces twenty to one.[19] Furthermore, these two Communist countries half
encircle eastern Austria and are only twenty-
five miles from Vienna. During the later years
of the occupation, Western forces in Austria
numbered about 20,000, but could always have
been reinforced many times over in case of danger; furthermore, these forces were directly
backed by nations with a combined population of
about 250 million and with vast potential power.
Although this power remains an indirect deter-
rent, Austria, on the other hand, will in the
next few years scarcely be able to reinforce
her troops even in the face of an imminent
threat.

   Taken alone, the very considerable strategic
advantages to the Soviet bloc that resulted from
Austria's independence and neutrality would appear to have justified the decision: Nevertheless, the Soviets apparently had other objectives in mind as well.[20]

The Austrian Treaty and German Neutrality

   From the very beginning, the Soviets made no
attempt to disguise the fact that they also regarded the State Treaty as a means to lure Western Germany into neutralism and away from her

newly formed military alliance with NATO and the
Western European Union. On April 18, 1955, Radio Moscow unequivocally stated: "If Bonn would
follow the Austrian example, Germany as a nation
and world peace would gain considerably." On
May 19, 1955, *Tägliche Rundschau*, the Soviet
daily for East Germany, affirmed that "Austria's
course can also be Germany's course" (*"Der Weg
Österreichs kann auch der Weg Deutschlands wer-
den"*). Furthermore, Molotov's references to the
German problem when the State Treaty was signed
were generally interpreted as an appeal to West
Germany to follow Austria's example.[21]

The effect on public opinion in West Germany
of the Soviet Union's changed policy towards
Austria was felt as soon as Raab returned from
Moscow, and some Germans were asking: "If Raab,
why not Adenauer? if Austria, why not Germany?"[22] On April 23, 1955, the *Frankfurter Allgemeine Zeitung* published a statement by a
spokesman of the West German federal government
to the effect that fundamental differences between Austria and Germany in size, location, and
status ruled out Austria as a model for Germany.
On May 20, 1955, the federal German government
announced that it was opposed to all plans for
neutralizing Germany since it would be dangerous
to Germany to reject a security system that included the United States.[23] On the same day,
French Foreign Minister Pinay announced that
France, the United States, and Great Britain
would reject all Soviet proposals for the neutralization of a reunified Germany.[24] A similar
declaration, on behalf of the United States, was
made by Dulles on May 24. In Germany, not only
the federal government, but also the major opposition party, the German Democratic party, opposed neutralization of Germany.[25] Initially,
at least, it appeared as though neutrality on
the Austrian pattern had less appeal to the

Germans than the Soviets had counted on. Molotov's hope that "other states will follow the
pattern" of Austria's neutrality might have indicated a broader Soviet desire to establish a
neutral belt across Europe that would include
Yugoslavia, Austria, West Germany, Sweden, and
Finland.[26] However, any hopes on the Western
side that neutrality might also apply to the
Soviet satellites in Europe were soon dashed by
a lead editorial in the Moscow *Pravda* of May 22,
1955, which labeled suggested changes in the
status of these states as "absolute nonsense."[27]

An Austrian view of the application of the
Austrian solution to other countries was expressed by Foreign Minister Dr. Bruno Kreisky
in a speech in Zurich on May 4, 1960:

*...nowhere, since 1955, can one find a clear
statement by a responsible Soviet statesman in-
dicating that the neutrality of Germany would
lead to reunification. I still remember very
well a comment by one of the most important
personalities in the Kremlin who...told me that
relations with a country of seven million can
be regulated [sich ordnen lassen] by a...treaty
document, but in the case of a country of seventy million relations are not so easily arranged
[regeln]. The example of Austria has misled
[verleitet] many political observers into believing that neutrality, as such, could possibly be brought in everywhere in all situations
to solve outstanding world problems. We believe
that, contrary to these views, the neutrality of
a country—as far as it can be accepted in agreement with both great power groups—is, like disarmament, only possible when it doesn't result
in a change in the international political balance [weltpolitischer Gleichgewichtszustand].
This alone is not enough. A policy of neutrality is a state's expression of will [Willens-*

äusserung]. *Today it can hardly be imposed on
a large country from without...this, of course,
could be done at a time of national weakness, but
no one could, without belligerent intervention
[kriegerische Intervention], prevent this state...
from deciding on a change in its basic policy.*[28]

In this connection it should be noted that no-
where is neutrality mentioned in the State Treaty,
since this was an obligation freely taken by Austria and not imposed upon her by the four occupying powers.

The Austrian Treaty and the "Spirit of Geneva"

On the day the treaty was signed, Vienna's *Die
Presse* realistically appraised this event as "the
opening move in a large concept [*Konzept*]" on the
part of the Soviet Union. On the previous day,
the Big Four foreign ministers had agreed to a
summit meeting of their respective chiefs of
state. President Eisenhower had always made his
attendance at such a meeting dependent on measures taken on the part of the Soviets to help resolve a number of outstanding sources of international friction, which the president enumerated
on April 16, 1953, and which included the signing of an Austrian treaty.[29] Taking this factor
into consideration, the signing of the Austrian
treaty played an important part in the U.S. decision to agree to this unfortunate meeting,
which was held in Geneva in July 1955.[30]
On May 13, 1955, *Izvestia* announced that Soviet
Premier Bulganin and Communist party chief
Khrushchev were going to Belgrade for a conference with Yugoslav President Tito, who had been
one of the Soviet bloc's archenemies between
1948 and the death of Stalin.[31] This startling
new Soviet mobility and initiative, which began

with the Austrian treaty, was further manifested
in: the propaganda exploitation of the superficial détente, the "Spirit of Geneva," which
resulted from the July summit meeting; the much-
publicized "reductions" of Soviet and satellite
armed forces; the Adenauer visit to Moscow, followed by the establishment of diplomatic relations with West Germany and the repatriation of
German prisoners of war; the handing back to
Finland of the Porkkala naval base; and the India
trip of Bulganin and Khrushchev. In 1956 its
manifestations included: the attempt at the Moscow Twentieth Party Congress to blame the evils
of Soviet Communism on Stalin, followed by the
dissolution of the Cominform and the Khrushchev
and Bulganin visit to Great Britain.[32]

Viewed in this context, the Austrian treaty,
among other things, appears indeed to have been
the gambit in a wide-scale Soviet plan to convince the non-Communist world that Soviet foreign
policy had undergone such a basic transformation
since the death of Stalin that the West no longer
had anything to fear and could safely dispense
with the irksome and expensive burdens of defense
and the obligations of military alliances.[33]

The Hungarian Revolution, however, destroyed
any chances of success this "peace offensive"
might have had.

Western Gains

Two days after the signing of the State Treaty,
Secretary of State Dulles, in a televised dialogue with President Eisenhower, stated:

*...Now, a lot of people are trying to find mys-
terious reasons why the Soviets changed their
policy. And that's something that, of course,
deserves the very careful thought that we're
giving it....But there are certain implications*

*of it that we can be quite sure of as far as our-
selves and which, I think, we can take great
satisfaction from. In the first place, it marks
the first time that the Red armies will have
turned their face in the other direction and
gone back since 1945....Now, that's bound to
have a tremendous impact in the other countries
where the Red armies are there in occupation.
It is going to create a desire—a mounting desire—on the part of those people to get the same
freedom from that type of occupation that the
Austrians have gotten. And furthermore this,
this joy at their freedom which was so manifest
by the Austrian people, that is going to be contagious, and it's going to spread surely to the
neighboring countries—Czechoslovakia—for the
first time there'll be an open door to freedom
on the part of Hungary....The Soviets are ac-
cepting those consequences. Why they are doing
it we're not quite sure, except we can be quite
certain that the policies of strength and firmness that we're adopting in partnership with
the other free countries of Europe are beginning to pay off and the people in Austria are
the first to say—and all of them did say to me—
this is a first dividend from the creation of
Western European unity and the bringing of Germany into NATO. Now, at the time when that was
under debate, the Soviet Union was threatening
terrible things would happen if we went through
with this. But we and the other free countries
of Europe did go through with it, and we find
that the payoff is not a terrible disaster, but
for the first time an apparent softening of
Soviet policy and a willingness to give greater
freedom and liberty to the captive satellite
peoples....I said to a group I was talking to
Vienna Sunday, I said it isn't so important to
speculate, really, as to who's winning, whether
the Soviet Union is winning or the United States*

*is winning. I said the important thing is that
sound principles are going...to prevail. If
we're behind them, then we'll automatically get
the benefit of prevailing....[N.Y. Times, May 18,
1955]*

On the following day, May 18, Vice-Chancellor
Schärf supported Secretary Dulles's major theme
in a broadcast over the Bavarian Radio Network in
which he stated that "the realization of the European defense community treaties created an entire-
ly new situation, which led to a greater willingness on the part of the Soviets to meet Austria
half way in new Treaty negotiations."[34]

Whereas the Soviet advantages derived from the
State Treaty were, for the most part, of a long-
range, speculative nature, the gains of the West
were immediate. For the first time since 1945,
the Soviet troops in Europe withdrew from their
positions of farthest wartime advance. In some
cases this withdrawal to the east was nearly 150
miles. Nearly 16,000 square miles and 1,700,000
people (not including the area and population of
the Soviet sector of Vienna) were freed from Soviet control and direct economic exploitation,
and the entire country got rid of the quadripartite controls kept in force at Soviet insistence.
Austria was also no longer threatened with partition and other dangers that would have directly involved the Western powers in a serious conflict.

In conclusion, it must be stated that Austria
played a decisive role in achieving her own
freedom. Were it not for the courage, vision,
and common sense of her leading statesmen in 1945
and during the periods of peril that followed, it
is highly questionable whether or not Austria
would have survived in her present form or could
have finally attained complete freedom. Without
the support of the overwhelming majority of the

population, Austria's leaders could have accomplished little. The outstanding role of the Austrian workers has already been described, but high praise is deserved by all those segments of the population who, by their clear and consistent orientation, contributed to the final achievement of independence.

Notes

1. See Stearman, *Soviet Union*, pp. 30, 160. Ygael Gluckstein, *Stalin's Satellites in Europe* (Boston: Beacon Press, 1952), p. 136; Ferenc Nagy, *The Struggle Behind the Iron Curtain* (New York: Macmillan, 1949); most of his book is devoted to this subject.

2. Cary T. Grayson, Jr., *Austria's International Position, 1938–1953* (Geneva: Librairie E. Droz, 1953), p. 169; John MacCormac *New York Times* report of March 9, 1950. See chapter 3 of Stearman, *Soviet Union*.

3. *Wiener Zeitung* (Vienna), February 3, 1952.

4. *The Rehabilitation of Austria*, 2:37–41, 52–59, 88.

5. Because the Soviets felt they had more to gain from an integrated Austria under a functioning quadripartite control, they were generally careful not to jeopardize this arrangement by violating the letter of the quadripartite agreements. When they did, they nearly always took pains to cloak their transgressions in legal justifications. Richard Hiscocks, *Rebirth of Austria* (London: Oxford University Press, 1953), p. 209.

6. John MacCormac reports to the *New York Times* of March 9, 1950, September 28, 1952, and October 2, 1952.

7. Harry Schwartz in the *New York Times* of
May 2, 1955; *Die Presse* (Vienna), May 15, 1955.

8. Karl Gruber, *Zwischen Befreiung und Freiheit* (Vienna: Ullstein Verlag, 1953), pp. 308-9.
See also Stearman, *Soviet Union*, p. 145, n. 58.
Chancellor Raab reportedly believed that the Soviets actually became interested in the possibility of a neutral Austria at the 1954 Berlin Conference. *Die Presse* (Vienna), May 19, 1955.
Bruno Kreisky, "Die österreichische Neutralität," in *Aktuelle Probleme unserer Zeit*, no. 5
(Vienna: Verlag des österreichischen Gewerk-
schaftsbundes, 1960), p. 11. Because neutrality
was freely chosen by Austria, there is no mention of it in the State Treaty.

9. *TASS*, February 8, 1955.

10. Between September 28 and October 3, 1954,
six Western European nations met with the United
States, Great Britain, and Canada in London to
work out an alternative to the European Defense
Community agreement for the integration of West
Germany into Western defense and the restoration
of her sovereignty—a plan that had been rejected
by the French National Assembly a month before.
As a result of this conference it was agreed
that the Brussels Pact of 1948 would be enlarged
to include the Federal Republic of Germany and
Italy. Between October 19 and 23, a series of
agreements was signed in Paris on the Saar territory; the restoration of West German sovereignty; the admission of Italy and West Germany to
the newly formed "Western European Union," the
expanded Brussels Pact; and the admission of the
Federal Republic of Germany to the North Atlantic
Treaty Organization.

11. *TASS*, December 2, 1954. The threat to form
an Eastern counterpart to NATO did not have too
much significance, since the Soviet Union was

already in de facto control of the satellite armed forces, and by March 1948 had concluded bilateral military pacts with Czechoslovakia, Poland, Bulgaria, Hungary, and Rumania. The satellites, in turn, were all linked by another series of bilateral pacts.

Austria—like Finland, Switzerland, and Yugoslavia—officially rejected the invitation to the Moscow conference because not all the interested parties to such discussions would be present. *Wiener Zeitung* (Vienna), November 28, 1954.

12. See Stearman, *Soviet Union*, pp. 147-48. At this time, even the most optimistic observers in Vienna did not believe that there would be further Four-Power talks on Austria until the Paris Agreements were ratified (*Die Neue Zeitung* [Berlin], January 20, 1955).

At the 1954 Berlin Conference Molotov had stated that if plans for the European Defense Community were withdrawn, "that would facilitate the conclusion of the solution of the question of the Austrian treaty." Foreign Ministers Meeting, Berlin Discussions, January 25 to February 18, 1954. Department of State Publication 5399 (Washington, D.C.: U.S. Government Printing Office, 1954), p. 197.

13. See Stearman, *Soviet Union*, pp. 148-49. Communist propaganda later carried this reversal even further by alleging that Secretary Dulles had believed that the ratification of the Paris Agreements would thwart the Austrian treaty, but that, nevertheless, the Soviets had led treaty negotiations to a successful conclusion. *Neues Deutschland* (East Berlin), May 14, 1955.

14. *TASS* (Warsaw), May 14, 1955. See also Stearman, *Soviet Union*, p. 161, n. 11.

15. For official Rumanian and Hungarian views favoring the continued stationing of Soviet troops

in these countries after the Austrian treaty,
see *Scinteia* (Bucharest), of August 12, 1955,
and *Zala* (Zalaegerszeg, Hungary), of June 7,
1955.

16. The Warsaw *Nowe Drogi* (no. 5, May 1955)
more specifically indicated that the treaty would
split NATO. The Soviet army publication *Krasnaya
Svesda* (Moscow) of March 23, 1955, referred to
the importance of western Austria to the Western
European Union. For years, Soviet propaganda had
harped on the importance of western Austria to
NATO (see Stearman, *Soviet Union*, p. 100). For
example, a lead editorial in the Soviet *Österreichische Zeitung* (Vienna) of December 12, 1953,
stressed the strategic importance of western Austria as a link between West Germany and Italy.
On June 7, 1960, Khrushchev declared in Klagenfurt that "should foreign rocket bases in Northern Italy be used against socialist countries,"
this would be a violation of Austria's neutrality. *TASS* (Klagenfurt), July 7, 1960.

17. *New York Times*, May 3, 1955; Adelbert
Weinstein, "Druckpunkte der österreichischen Verteidigung," *Frankfurter Allgemeine Zeitung* (Frank-
furt), June 13, 1957. The problems posed by Austria's neutrality were very much in evidence during the Lebanon crisis in the summer of 1958,
when it became necessary to fly American military aircraft to the Near East from West Germany.
See Stearman, *Soviet Union*, p. 235, n. 23.

18. *Neue Zürcher Zeitung* (Zurich), May 5,
1955; *Die Presse* (Vienna), May 16, 1955.

19. *New York Times*, March 25, 1956; *Die Presse*
(Vienna), January 24, 1956, and June 19, 1955.

20. The strategic significance of Austrian
neutrality might be depreciated by atomic-age
strategists in the West who would argue that such

geographical disadvantages mean little in view
of the existence of ballistics missiles with
ranges from hundreds to thousands of miles. The
Soviet military doctrine, on the other hand,
plans to a greater extent for both conventional
and nuclear warfare and is opposed to placing
too much emphasis on any one strategic concept.
Raymond L. Garthoff, *Soviet Military Doctrine*
(Glencoe, Ill.: Free Press, 1953), pp. 173-77.

21. "...Austria has declared she will maintain permanent neutrality and now there will be
in Central Europe, neighboring Switzerland, a
neutral Austria....Allow me to express the conviction that other states will also follow the
pattern....The Soviet Union will go on trying to
find ways for a peaceful and democratic settlement of the German question which would correspond to the legitimate efforts of the German
people for reestablishing their unity without
reviving their militarism...." Molotov quoted
from the *New York Times*, May 16, 1955.

The Soviet note to the government of the Federal Republic of Germany of September 18, 1958,
on a peace treaty pointed out that the conclusion of the Austrian State Treaty showed what a
state could accomplish when it contributed to
the solution of questions of vital importance
to it. *Die Sowjetunion heute* (Soviet Embassy,
Bonn), no. 28 (October 1, 1958, insert). This
also implied advantages in dealing directly with
the Soviet Union (or East Germany) on a treaty,
as the Austrians had done. In notes of March 10,
1952, and January 10, 1959, the Soviet government had proposed a neutral status for the Federal Republic of Germany. At a press conference
in Vienna on July 8, 1960, Khrushchev declared:
"If the Governments of the Federal Republic of
Germany and the German Democratic Republic would
declare the neutrality of their states, this

would be a great satisfaction to all the peoples
of the world. We ourselves would welcome and
respect this neutrality." *Die Sowjetunion heute*
(Soviet Embassy, Bonn), no. 20, July 10, 1960,
p. 21.

22. *Neue Zürcher Zeitung* (Zurich), April 22,
1955.

23. *Frankfurter Allgemeine Zeitung* (Frank-
furt), May 21, 1955.

24. United Press, Paris, May 20, 1955.

25. Speech of the chairman of the Social
Democratic party, Erich Ollenhauer, over the
Bavarian Radio network on May 4, 1955.

26. *New York Times*, May 16, 1955. A West German journalist, Wolfgang Höpker, has developed
this thesis in his book *Europäisches Niemands-
land* (Dusseldorf and Cologne: Eugen Diederichs
Verlag, 1956).

It was apparent that Japan was also included
among the "other states" referred to by Molotov
when, on June 17, 1955, Soviet representatives
in London offered Japan a treaty which would bar
any "alliance or military coalitions directed
against any power that fought against Japan in
World War II." *New York Times*, June 17, 1955.

27. The Czechoslovakian *Pravda* (Bratislava)
of September 13, 1955, scorned the idea of neutralizing the "Eastern European countries," and
declared: "The proclamation of neutrality for a
socialist state (if this were possible at all)
would mean a step backwards, from active to passive peace politics" (Foreign Broadcast Information Service translation). *Kommunist*, the important organ of Soviet Communist theory made
the following pronouncement on neutrality for
Communist countries: "It is clear that in the
present situation neutrality declared by a

bourgeois state indicates a progressive attitude which strengthens world peace. It is likewise clear that in a period in which a violent class struggle rages in the world arena, 'neutrality' in the class struggle between socialism and capitalism is, for a country that regards itself as socialist, synonymous with opposing and damaging the friendly cooperation of the socialist countries." V. Cherpakov, "Always Deeper into the Revisionistic Morass," *Kommunist*, no. 18 (December 1958), p. 108.

Considerably less subtle was the Soviet Union's reply to Hungary's 1956 attempt to become neutral. See Stearman, *Soviet Union*, p. 174.

In February 1957, the first secretary of the Socialist (Communist) Unity party in Magdeburg, Alois Pitnik, complained that party members were exhibiting "revisionist and counter-revolutionary ideas" and cited as an example proposals in one large factory that East Germany should bolt the Soviet camp and become "neutral like Austria." Associated Press, Berlin, February 17, 1957. See note 21 above, for Khrushchev's 1960 views on East German neutrality.

28.   Kreisky, "Die österreichische Neutralität," p. 11.

29. *New York Times*, April 27, 1953, January 8, 1954, and May 18, 1955 (Dulles-Eisenhower dialogue).

30. A summit conference was originally proposed by Sir Winston Churchill on May 11, 1953, and the idea was later taken up by the Soviets; Molotov stated on October 21, 1953, that "Vienna was a good basis [*Voraussetzung*] for Geneva." *Die Presse* (Vienna), October 25, 1955. For Western criticisms of the Geneva summit conference of 1955 see: James Reston, *New York Times*, April 19, 1956; British Broadcasting Corporation interview with Secretary Dulles, 2115 hours GMT, December 3,

1957; Michael T. Florinsky, "The USSR and Western
Europe," *Current History*, February 1957, pp. 79-80.

31. *New York Times*, May 14, 1955. The Soviets
indicated that the successful Austro-Soviet negotiations of April 1955 offer the countries of
southeast Europe the possibility of political,
commercial, and cultural cooperation, and stressed
the favorable reception these negotiations received in Yugoslavia. "Was die sowjetisch-öster-
reichischen Verhandlungen in Moskau gezeigt haben,"
Neue Zeit (Moscow), no. 17 (April 23, 1955), pp. 1-2.

32. The more venturesome and imaginative foreign policy pursued by the Soviet Union in 1955
was clearly the work of Nikita Khrushchev. Reportedly his most daring foreign policy moves,
the Austrian treaty and the rapprochement with
Tito, were opposed by Molotov, who advocated a
more rigid approach. This was reported by Harri-
son E. Salisbury in the *New York Times* of April
20, 1956, and was announced by Radio Moscow on
July 3, 1957.

The point at which Khrushchev gained primary
control over Soviet foreign policy is difficult
to determine, and in the beginning, at least,
foreign-policy decisions might well have been influenced by several members of the Party presi-
dium. Khrushchev's increasing voice in foreign
policy first became evident when, on October 1,
1954, he (and not Molotov) went to Peiping on a
major diplomatic mission to regulate differences
between the Soviet Union and Red China. By the
end of 1954, Khrushchev had clearly overcome his
major political rival, Malenkov, and was, by
then, probably the chief architect of Soviet foreign policy. *New York Times*, March 10, 1958;
Myron Rush, *The Rise of Khrushchev* (Washington,
D.C.: Public Affairs Press, 1958), p. 23.

The overt rivalry between Malenkov and Khrushchev manifested itself in a dispute over the

primacy of heavy industry, which the latter favored. When, on December 28, 1954, most of the
leading Moscow dailies carried an outspoken
Khrushchev attack on Malenkov's economic theo-
ries, it was somewhat evident that the latter's
political fate was sealed. On February 8, 1955,
he asked to be relieved of his position as premier, and Khrushchev named Bulganin to replace
him. See Stearman, *Soviet Union*, p. 149.

There were reports from Austrian sources that
an attempt had been made in mid-1954, before
Khrushchev had consolidated his position, to ini-
tiate a settlement of the Austrian question, but
it had been held up due to internal differences
(*Neue Zürcher Zeitung* [*Zurich*], *April 18, 1955*).

33. Khrushchev reportedly told a French Communist delegation visiting Moscow in mid-1956: "This
criticism [of Stalin], this elimination of past
errors, cannot fail to strengthen the USSR and
make Soviet foreign policy more attractive in the
eyes of people all over the world" (*New York Her-
ald Tribune*, European edition, July 20, 1956).
Radio Moscow broadcast on July 3, 1957: "The conclusion of the Austrian treaty was largely instrumental in lessening international tensions in
general."

The Icelandic parliament, on March 28, 1956,
passed a resolution which, "in view of the changed
situation," called for the withdrawal of U.S.
troops (manning a vital strategic airbase) sta-
tioned in Iceland under the terms of the U.S.-
Iceland defense agreement of 1951. Iceland has
no defense forces of her own to defend this
strategically important island (*New York Times*,
March 30, 1956). Commenting on the Iceland
situation before a Senate subcommittee, Gen.
Omar Bradley, former U.S. chief of staff, stated:
"I am concerned also because Russian propaganda
is having an effect on the integrity of NATO"
(*New York Times*, April 17, 1956).

Commenting on the same situation, *Izvestia*
(Moscow) of April 1, 1956, observed that there
had recently been pressure in the NATO countries
for a "revision of the Atlantic policy" and that
"the decision of the Icelandic Parliament must
naturally be viewed in relation to this whole development....In the course of time more and more
Icelanders became convinced that there was no
Soviet danger...."
Under the impact of the Soviet suppression of
the Hungarian uprising in October and November of
1956, however, the Icelandic parliament in December 1956 withdrew its request for the evacuation
of American troops.

34. Similar opinions were also expressed by
Minister of Interior Helmer, who was equally
realistic and experienced (*Die Zukunft* [Vienna]
12 [December 1955]:341). Actually, the theory
that the Austrian Treaty came about as a result
of the Paris Agreements was indirectly confirmed
by Soviet and other Communist statements. For
example, Molotov's statements of February 8, 1955,
on the Austrian problem clearly indicated that
the probable ratification of the Paris Agreements
had altered the Soviet Union's position on the
State Treaty. (See Stearman, *Soviet Union*,
pp. 148, 162.) Even more specific was an article
in the organ of the Central Committee of the
Polish Worker's [Communist] party, *Nowe Drogi*
(Warsaw), no. 5, May 1955, which stated:

*The ratification of the Paris Agreements and the
remilitarization of West Germany has created a
new situation which, for the time being, makes
the reunification of Germany and the conclusion
of a peace treaty with this country impossible.
The Austrian people saw itself threatened with
an indefinite postponement of the conclusion of
the State Treaty. At the same time this country*

*was defenseless against the revival of milita-
rism.   Under these circumstances, the Government
of the Soviet Union made a constructive new proposal.   In the session of the Supreme Soviet,
Minister Molotov, on February 8, 1955, declared
that one could forego linking the Austrian and
German questions if in some other manner sufficient guarantees against an Anschluss are given.*
(Author's translation.)

MANFRIED RAUCHENSTEINER

Austria under
Allied Occupation between
1945 and 1955

A Historical Review

Undoubtedly the time of occupation has become the most important period in the history of the Second Austrian Republic. This is so not only because of the dramatic beginning and the no-less-dramatic end of that period, but particularly because of the events that occurred during that period. This is revealed in full depth by recent historical research that was of special prominence in 1980, when Austria celebrated the twenty-fifth anniversary of the end of the occupation period. Historians and politicians in East and West have described the period of occupation as having its own phenomenology and as being something special in the era of the so-called cold war. To assume that Austria would be different had she not undergone the time of occupation is a mere hypothesis. Nonetheless, it could be extended, and one could say that Europe would be different too. Therefore, Austria under Allied occupation is a subject of European and international history. To prove that, let us put our first sounding question: How did it all come about?

The answer is easy if one recalls the situation of those armies that closed in on Austria in March and April 1945. But this is only part

of the story because the considerations of the
Allies—why, how, and with what intention Austria
(a still nonexistent Austria) should be occupied—must at least be mentioned briefly in this
connection. Austria—at least after the Moscow
Declaration of November 1, 1943—was intended to
be reestablished as a free and independent state
patterned after the First Republic, but that
Austria was still a theoretical entity. All the
officials who discussed the reestablishment of
Austria in consultations among the Allies sooner
or later found themselves in the uneasy position
of speaking about something that only existed as
a theoretical entity—an entity that perhaps would
have to be created and that in the end would turn
out to be not viable at all.

Thus, it seemed to be much easier to discuss
possible ways of dividing Austria in accordance
with its earlier boundaries. Talks to that effect were also held after the Moscow Declaration.
Basically, Austria was occupied under the still
very strong reservation that one would have to
see if that state could be reestablished or if a
completely different solution would have to be
found. Both a partition and a reestablishment
of Austria were discussed, and one must understand—though with disapproval—that politicians
of the Western Allies in particular often noted
that one should more or less disregard the wishes
of the people concerned in favor of establishing
a lasting political solution.

The inability to foresee future developments
and their implications may have been the reason
why the Allies negotiated in the European Advisory Commission in London for more than one
and a half years about how to occupy Austria.
This was three quarters of a year longer than the
negotiations concerning Germany. The military
execution of the plan was not the problem. The
questions were if and how Austria should be

divided into zones of occupation like Germany
and how the Allies should exert their unre-
stricted power of control stemming from an unconditional surrender. When, about two months
after the end of the war, the first Control Agreement and the agreement on zones of occupation in
Austria had been jointly agreed upon by the Allies—the agreements are dated July 4, 1945, and
July 9, 1945, respectively—two options were still
left open.

If the Austrian experiment failed, something
else would have to take its place. If it succeeded, one could conclude further agreements as
required. Thus, it was largely left to Austria
and to her leading politicians—one could call
them the *Patres Patriae* of modern Austria—to
prove that a new Austria would be a viable one.
This had to be done under aggravating circumstances—under total occupation, with a strict
division into zones of occupation, largely isolated from the international community, and under
the conditions of want and squalor.

Practically nothing could be done by anyone in
Austria without falling under the jurisdiction
of an occupying force and thus requiring its respective consent. The difficulties of a new
start were increased by the fact that each of the
occupying forces had its own model of occupation,
which it was eager to apply. The Soviet model
envisaged the building of an administration from
the top to the bottom, whereas the Anglo-American
model was designed to work from the grass roots
upward. That divergence proved to be the first
challenge. When, upon Soviet demand, Karl Renner
presented his cabinet on April 27, he not only
aroused Western suspicions that the Soviets could
try to "Sovietize" Austria, he also unknowingly
disregarded the Western model of occupation. It
turned out to be the resistance of bureaucrats—
especially British bureaucrats, who had designed

the Western model and who wanted to try it out
in practice at any price—that gave Renner and
his provisional government a hard time. Renner
decisively influenced this initial phase. He
used the mandate that had been given to him by
part of the Soviet occupying force (initially
only by the commander in charge of the area south
of the Danube) in such a clever way that he was
able to extend the authority of his government,
which in the beginning only comprised Vienna, to
the rest of the country. He was able to make his
government attractive to the Western Allies as
well, so that their bureaucratic rejection did
not become a crucial matter for the existence of
Austria.

The Allies were sufficiently intrigued by Renner that he was at least given a chance. Nevertheless, the provisional government and the provisional authorities of provinces, counties, and
communities were put under the complete control
of the Allied Council that convened for its first
session in Vienna on September 11, 1945. It took
over the supreme authority and at the same time
drastically cut the aspirations of the Renner
government for jurisdiction.

The provisional government was put in the situation of having to achieve the impossible: On the
one hand, it had to demonstrate its ability to
exert unlimited power in order to be recognized
by the Allies; on the other hand, it was necessary to demonstrate—at least symbolically—its
ability and willingness to oppose the Allies in
order to gain recognition internally.

Austria demonstrated an unexpectedly high degree of ability for reconstruction, which in one
way or another was also appreciated by the victorious nations. They finally accepted and took
part in the formulation that Austria had been
the first victim of National Socialism; a belief
against which some reservations have been voiced.

The Allies went on with negotiations about Austria.

Although Austria itself was considered to be a separate entity, the only solution found to be feasible was breaking up the country into occupation zones like those in Germany. This was decided upon in spite of the original intention to treat Austria differently—and better—than Germany. Such treatment, however, could only take place under two conditions:

1. a minimal consensus of the victors on the question of Austria

2. Austrian ability to reconstruct and restore.

The first free elections on November 25, 1945, marked the end of the immediate restoration process. From that time onward, Austria worked toward ending the occupation. Austria had been willing to accept the presence of Allied forces, Allied control, and a strong Allied influence in the process of restoration in the fields of politics, administration, and economy as a necessary consequence of liberation. But as time wore on, one would have to ask why the occupation still persisted.

It is worth noting that in the early stages of the discussion (1942-45) on a continued occupation of Austria, it had not been envisaged that Austria would be occupied until a peace treaty or a state treaty had been signed. It was later argued, however, that this had been the undisputed intention.

By the end of 1945 the Allies started to think over their position on a long-term policy on Austria. It was obvious that their deliberations were based on the assumption that the Austrian experiment had been a successful one and that none of the occupying forces had an immediate

strategic interest in Austria. This was a very
important point. But they found no real opportunity for a complete withdrawal from Austria
because a number of economic questions remained
unsettled and because of a rising distrust.

That distrust was not the one that might have
been expected to exist between the Soviet and
the U.S. commanders in chief in Austria. It was,
instead, a repercussion from the disintegration
of a united front among the Allies themselves.

At that time a special atmosphere began to develop: Irrespective of difficulties in the international sphere, notwithstanding the differences and incidents resulting from daily routine
during the time of occupation, and regardless of
different opinions concerning Austrian matters,
the Allies kept up their willingness to negotiate.
Furthermore, over the course of the years, the
Allied Council developed into a body of concilia-
tion and understanding that took on special significance during times of increased tensions—as
in 1947, 1948, and also in 1950, when the Allied
Council provided an unusually good climate for
negotiations. This does not at all imply that
the Soviet general would have disregarded Moscow
or that his U.S. counterpart would have disregarded Washington. But the fact that Austria
was not part of any sphere of influence helped
quite a bit in the talks and enabled the negotiators to stay away from extreme positions.

The first and very efficient step towards a
qualitative change in the occupation of Austria
was the beginning of negotiations in the Allied
Council on a new control agreement in February
1946. The old agreement had left open the option to reduce the degree of control if certain
conditions were met. The most important condition was the de jure recognition of an Austrian
government, a condition that already had been
met. Negotiations were also started on how the

Allies could reduce their degree of control
without (and this was their basic reservation)
granting Austria her full sovereignty. All
four powers unanimously wished to keep the
supreme power amongst themselves.

But there was another special problem. Negotiations had been going on since autumn 1945
concerning how the Soviets could assert their
legal claim in regard to German property, a claim
that had been awarded to them at the Potsdam Conference for Austria. This claim had caused severe differences in opinion between the U.S. and
the USSR, since in the meantime the Americans had
realized the enormous disadvantages that could
have arisen from a Soviet takeover of German property. Negotiations on that problem ended in a
deadlock.

The happy thought of the second control agreement was to concede the German property to the
Russians more or less tacitly and at the same
time to drastically reduce the amount of Allied
control. That is exactly what happened. As a
consequence of the second control agreement, the
Allies themselves reduced their right to veto
Austrian legislation; less important bills were
no longer subject to Allied approval—if the bill
in question had not been vetoed within thirty-
one days, it automatically became law. The only
exception to that rule were bills of constitutional content.

Compared with these qualitative changes, the
quantitative aspect lost its importance. The occupying forces reduced their troop strength considerably in 1946. It fell from 337,000 in
December 1945 to less than 100,000 in December
1946. But the sheer size of the occupying forces
was not that important in itself; it only served
as a carefully observed indicator of whether any
of the occupying powers intended to support a
political demand with a military threat. One

can now confidently state that at no time between
1945 and 1955 was a military option considered
by any of the occupying powers.

The time of occupation may be divided into two
periods. The first, after the actual taking of
the country, was marked by the establishment of
total control. It was followed by the second
period, which was characterized by less strict
control. The duration of the first period had
not been defined precisely; it ended, however,
in June 1946. According to the second Control
Agreement, the second period had been slated to
last for six months, but in fact it lasted until
1955.

This period also saw some qualitative changes—
though they were not that spectacular in comparison with those that resulted from the second Control Agreement, the importance of which
seems to be underestimated by Austrian historians. Without the second Control Agreement,
however, there could have been a real danger of
a division of the country. Such a division would
have been caused by one or a number of occupation
zones attempting to improve their position by
taking into account the political climate of that
time, and not at the instigation of an occupier.
The importance of the second Control Agreement
was also to safeguard Austrian self-administra-
tion to such a degree as to make it possible to
ward off outside influences if necessary. It
also gave time to the Austrians to patiently
negotiate the Austrian State Treaty. Without
the second Control Agreement, any failure in
these negotiations would have returned Austria
to the yoke of total control; such a state of
affairs would not have just caused disappointment, it would have created utter despair. Obviously the negotiations leading to the State
Treaty strongly influenced the qualitative
changes during the time of occupation. The

stipulations of that treaty, as agreed upon step by step, were in themselves an indicator of the prestige of a future Austria and had their bearing on Austria as it then existed. The imminent signing of a treaty—as hoped for in 1947, as visible in 1948, and as almost tangible in 1949—also led to changes in the occupying forces. That could mean reduced troop strengths or easier procedures in the dealings between representatives of the occupying forces and the Austrians. Even deadlocks in the negotiations had their positive aspects. In particular, the U.S. initiated improvements at each of these occasions in order to compensate for the unavoidable disappointment to the Austrian side.

After the 1947 conference of foreign ministers in Moscow, the U.S. waived the further payment of stationing costs and even returned the contributions paid until then. From that time onwards, the occupation by the U.S. was a noncost operation. The other three occupying powers still insisted on a continued payment of stationing costs. In 1948, when the negotiations on a state treaty had not yet yielded any result, the U.S. could point out that it had been possible for Austria to take part in the Marshall Plan, even though the U.S. had been aware that a certain amount of aid would go east and thus be lost. In 1949, when the negotiations once again ended in a deadlock, the U.S. envisaged the signing of a third control agreement. And in fact the Western Allies agreed to exchange the military high commissioners for civilian ones. This "civilianizing" process also meant a qualitative change.

From the entering into force of the second Control Agreement onwards, the measures taken by the Allies lost their uniformity. Each commander of a zone of occupation had the right to take unilateral steps within his zone, and this led

to often severe differences with the result that
the western part of Austria was accorded liberal
treatment while the Soviet zone of occupation
was very restrictive.   From 1947 on, the Western
powers ceased their checks at the borders of
their zones.   They abolished censorship, placed
the bulk of German property in their zones under
Austrian trusteeship, and took some other measures to contribute toward the normalization of
the situation.

In contrast, there were strict controls in the
Soviet zone of occupation and numerous infringe-
ments upon the rights of citizens, censorship
was enforced rigorously, and the special status
of the companies that were German property (now
Societ property in Austria)—including nearly the
entire Austrian oil industry—led to a difficult
situation.   There was simply no momentum that
could have led to an unhampered development.   In
the Soviet zone the military presence was also
much more obvious than in the Western zones;
44,000 Soviet soldiers are, of course, much more
visible than, for example, the 4,000 French soldiers that were spread over the provinces of
Vorarlberg and the Tyrol as well as in the
French zone in Vienna.

After the negotiations on a state treaty were
thwarted in 1950, the occupation of Austria
seemed to have been perpetuated indefinitely.
Austrian attempts to make the world powers and
the international community aware of the still
unsettled problem did not have any noticeable
effect until the summer of 1953.   At that time
the Soviets, in a belated action, waived the
payment of stationing costs, ceased their checks
at the borders of their zone, abolished censorship, and ended some other restrictions.   Finally, the troop strength was reduced once more.

This last event in the period of occupation
ushered in the phase of decisive negotiations on

the State Treaty. From summer 1953 onwards, the
concept of neutrality became clearer and clearer,
and it was brought forward in the negotiations.
The Berlin Conference of foreign ministers in
February 1954—when Austria was allowed for the
first time to take part in the negotiations instead of waiting outside the conference room—was
once again disappointing, but the prospects of a
final solution began to emerge. This final solution was achieved, as we know, at the Moscow
negotiations in April 1955, and at the final
State Treaty conference in May.

But the conclusion of the State Treaty itself
did not lead to an immediate end to the state
of occupation. It was only after the deposition
of the last instrument of ratification of the
State Treaty by France that the Allied Council
met for its concluding session and lifted the
second Control Agreement. It is interesting to
note that the Allied agreement on the division
of Austria into zones of occupation has never
been formally revoked; it simply was superseded
by the fact that foreign occupying forces had
left Austria by October 25, 1955.

To summarize the importance of the period of
occupation for the Austria of today, one can say
that it was a period that forced all Austrians
to cooperate closely and that it still has its
repercussions on present-day Austria.

The State Treaty and the Balance of Power in Europe

In 1980, Austria not only celebrated the
twenty-fifth anniversary of the signing in Vienna of the State Treaty and the restoration of
her sovereignty, the country also celebrated
twenty-five years of the new federal armed forces,
the *Bundesheer*. Both occasions give ample reason
to analyze the influence of the State Treaty and

neutrality on the Austrian armed forces and on
the balance of power in Europe as well.

The first indications during the decisive
State Treaty discussions in Moscow in April 1955
that Austria would renew its offer to become a
neutral state produced some negative comments in
the United States, because American politicians
and military experts were skeptical in regard to
the capability of Austria to defend such a neutral position. They advised their government to
be cautious, because at that time it was absolutely unpredictable how Austrian neutrality
would affect the overall situation in Europe.
Any American consent in favor of such neutrality
was based on the requirement that there be an
immediate buildup of Austrian armed forces. No
military vacuum should be created once the occupation forces left Austria.

Although Austria was not willing to start immediately with the creation of military formations in order to dispel American hesitations,
the country did do so in its own interests.
After the Soviet Union had accepted the Austrian
proposal to declare itself a neutral country
along Swiss lines, Austria asked for the elimination of certain restrictive clauses of the treaty. In the final round of the treaty discussions
this was accomplished.

Hence, Austria was able to create military
forces without numerical limitations. Conscrip-
tion and reserve forces training could be insti-
tuted. However, the State Treaty contained and
still contains severe limitations in regard to
so-called special weapons, e.g., missiles of all
kinds. Today this affects the defense posture
of Austria gravely. In 1955, however, there was
only one guiding factor: to end the foreign occupation as fast as possible. And this did happen.

The dominating importance of the State Treaty
and all questions within its context at that time
had at first obscured some more far-reaching per-
spectives. Let us look at some of them.

We must clearly state here that the treaty only
came about because Austria demonstrated its willingness to accede to the desire of the Soviet
Union that it assume a state of neutrality. The
Soviet Union was interested in a neutral Austria
because this would have strategic effects on
NATO. As you will remember, early in 1955 the
Federal Republic of Germany had joined NATO, and
because of this, NATO for the first time com-
manded sizable ground forces. As a countermove,
the USSR created the Warsaw Pact. The withdrawal
of all foreign troops from Austrian soil not only
created a neutral state but also had two other
consequences:

1. American and Soviet forces became more wide-
    ly separated in a crucial part of central
    Europe. Even today there are 90,000 Soviet
    soldiers stationed in Hungary, but they are
    not directly at the Austrian border.

2. A neutral Austria divided NATO into a north-
    ern and a southern part, separated by the
    neutral belt of Austria and Switzerland.

Therefore, it is evident that the neutrality of
Austria brought more advantages to the Soviet
Union than to NATO. This makes the early American reactions more understandable. But the
negative evaluations of the proposed Austrian
neutrality went farther, and even Switzerland
then judged a neutral Austria to be a strategic
risk, because all of central Europe would (at
least in the view of some Swiss commentators)
be destabilized in a certain way, threatening
also to Switzerland.

There is no question that Austria needed to prove that the permanent neutrality would have positive effects for all of Europe, and that Austria could be counted upon to make her contribution to the stabilization of Europe. To demonstrate this was certainly no easy task, however.

It was not fully understood in Austria how a neutral state could and should act politically. In the first years after 1945, neutrality was understood primarily in accordance with international law, i.e., no military agreements with foreign powers and no foreign troops and installations on Austrian territory. In addition, the need to create a defense system was recognized. The role of the army within the context of Austria's national security policy and of her neutrality was not very clear, however. There were several reasons for this problem:

1. In spite of a long military tradition, Austria's armies were directed until 1918 by the needs of a world power and not by the requirements of a small country's neutrality.

2. The existence of an army was generally judged to be a factor of influence in internal stability and party politics, and this seemed not very desirable.

3. Most of the wars Austria had fought in recent history had ended in military defeat.

4. In the Second World War, Austria lost nearly 250,000 soldiers serving in the German Wehrmacht.

5. Ten years of foreign occupation were partially based on the thesis that Austria should be totally demilitarized.

And now all this had to be forgotten suddenly!

Nevertheless, the change actually started as
early as 1955. It was evident even then that
Austria's neutrality, originally considered a
static element, had become a dynamic force.

As early as 1955 certain proposals were heard
in Czechoslovakia considering neutrality for that
country. And in 1956, we saw a revolution in Hungary that aimed at neutrality for that country as
well. We know very well that these attempts
failed; it was precisely these failures of its
neighbors to achieve neutrality, however, that
demonstrated quite dramatically to the Austrians
the significance of their own neutrality. At
least at that time all Europe became aware of
Austrian neutrality and its values.

We have come to see since then that Austria can
add more importance to its neutral position during periods of détente than during periods of
international tensions. When tensions exist,
however, Austria's defense forces enjoy increased
attention from abroad. Will and ability to defend oneself is an indicator how much outside
pressure Austria would be capable of withstand-
ing. During the invasion of Czechoslovakia by
Warsaw Pact armies in 1968, the Austrian forces
were alerted and were partially relocated to
eastern Austria. Certainly, 20,000 men ordered
to secure the northern border was not a very impressive force, but they fulfilled their role.

Maybe this particular incident contributed towards a fresh approach in reconsidering Austrian
neutrality. After 1968 Austria's neutrality
policy became an even more active and dynamic
one. It could very well be that this new political approach will eventually have its effect even
on Switzerland.

Austria is active in the United Nations and
participates in its peacekeeping operations,
especially during the last ten years, with troops
in the Near East. So far, more than 14,000

Austrian officers and soldiers have served in
various U.N. forces. This, I think, is quite a
dramatic figure for such a small country. Austria has also played quite an important part in
the Conference on Security and Cooperation in
Europe and has not only emphasized its position
as a neutral state but has made good use of a
historic asset: Although it is a Western democracy, Austria was for centuries united as one
empire with countries of south and southeast Europe. Certain bonds are still in existence from
these times and they enable Austria to understand
perhaps better than others how those countries
act and react politically.

After twenty-five years of neutrality, Austria
is more aware than ever before that its status
within the framework of international law is a
function of the balance of power in Europe. And
I can assure you that the Soviet Union is aware
of this too. When some of us Research Fellows
of the Vienna Museum of Military History were invited by the Soviet Academy of Sciences in Moscow
in the spring of 1980 the eminent strategist
Daniil M. Proektor asked us quite bluntly, if a
sudden imbalance within the European scene would
not make Austria's neutrality questionable. This
inquiry was aimed at NATO's decision to develop
and deploy in Western Europe a new generation of
tactical nuclear weapons. All we could answer
was that the balance of power in Europe could
definitely not be altered or influenced by Austria. All Austria can do is to show that it is
a constant and stable element in Europe and that
it is willing to defend itself if necessary with
all means available.

There was another question with a certain impact in Moscow: What would Austria do if NATO
were to install cruise missiles in northern Italy?
Such missiles would, our interlocutors indicated,
probably cross Austria's territory to reach their

targets in Eastern Europe, and that would surely
be considered a violation of the Austrian neutrality. Well frankly, these are problems beyond
Austria's present capabilities. Austria has forwarded a diplomatic note to Rome, stating that
Austria takes it for granted that cruise missiles,
when used, will not cross Austrian airspace.
Quite contrary to this apparent display of Soviet
compassion, however, when Austria attempted in
1980 to obtain the Soviet Union's consent to newly
interpret Article 13 of the State Treaty, which
excludes all kinds of missiles for the Austrian
forces, it was not too successful.

Let me conclude: Austria's neutrality is just
twenty-five years young. This neutrality is a
permanent one, based on international law, and
Austria will defend this neutrality. Furthermore,
for a quarter of a century Austria has been able
to prove that it has the desire to be a stabiliz-
ing factor in Europe and that it has fulfilled
the hopes that came along with its neutrality.

Let me make a final comparison. Austria as a
permanent neutral state, is like a cadmium rod
in a nuclear reactor: It regulates a peaceful
output of energy. If this cadmium rod is ever
removed, disaster is inevitable.

ROBERT G. NEUMANN

Austrian Neutrality–
Precursor of Détente?
Model for the Future?

Within the hallowed grounds of academe, language is used—or is presumably used—to clarify
thoughts and subjects; in politics and diplomacy, it is frequently employed to obscure both
these useful purposes in their respective
spheres. I should like to define certain terms
that are frequently used incorrectly or loosely:
neutrality, neutralism, and neutralization.

In classical international law, *neutrality* applied only when there existed a state of war—
usually declared war—between two or more parties, while other, third parties declared themselves neutral. This meant merely that the latter wished to take no part in the hostilities,
that they expected the belligerents to recognize their neutrality, and that they would in
turn accept those limitations on their own freedom of operation and commerce that the law of
war imposes on neutrals, such as the acceptance
of a legal blockade imposed by one belligerent
against another. Beyond the purely legal mean-
ing of the term, however, neutrality implies a
political decision by one country not to take
any part in the conflicts, belligerent or not,
between two other countries.

Neutralism is purely, or almost purely, a
political term that sometimes also is used to
mean a status of nonalignment or block-free

existence sponsored by various Third-World leaders, especially the late Indian Prime Minister
Jawaharlal Nehru, and inspired by the idea that
the countries not directly aligned with either
the U.S. or the USSR ought to form a third force
and establish cooperation and consultation among
one another, though preserving their individual
freedom to take positions on each issue as it
comes up. The fact that Cuba is a member, and
even a leading member, of this group indicates,
however, that the reality of this sort of "neutralism" is highly suspect, at least as far as
some members of the group are concerned.

Neutralization is an older, essentially legal
arrangement by which a country accepts, either
unilaterally or as part of a treaty or general
agreement, a certain limitation on its own action or sovereignty, precluding its entry into
an alliance or similar arrangement. Austria,
Sweden, and Switzerland are the principal and
most classic examples of neutralization. But
each of these three countries has a different
interpretation of its status and limitations,
with the result that Austria's interpretation
permits it a more activist position in international affairs than has been the case with Sweden
and especially with Switzerland.

Turning from the legal to the political, it may
be useful to point out that the Austrian State
Treaty of 1955 not only established the first
post-World War II act of neutralization, but also
constituted the first break in the cold war relations between East and West. Without that
event, it would have been quite difficult to move
on to the later period of détente.

This being the case, it is not surprising that
many observers look to that period and that
achievement with a certain nostalgia and ask the
question whether this Austrian model might not
apply to present and future problems, in particular to the sudden cooling of East-West relations

following the Soviet invasion of Afghanistan. I
welcome the opportunity to express myself on this
subject because it brings together both my Austrian origin and my experience as U.S. ambassador
to Afghanistan from 1966 to 1973.

In order to answer the question of the applicability of the Austrian model to the present Afghanistan crisis, we should examine for just a
moment the circumstances that made the 1955 Austrian State Treaty possible, in order to see
whether there are any parallels to the present
situation in and around Afghanistan.

The situation between the end of World War II
and 1955 is rather well-known, despite the amount
of nonsense written by revisionist historians.
Certainly it is clear to all those who lived con-
sciously and actively in that period that the
cold war started as an act primarily undertaken
by the Soviet Union, that it had its origin while
World War II was still in progress, and that this
fact was very clearly demonstrated by the Soviet
maneuvers leading to the total control of Poland
and to the charade of allegedly quadripartite
control of Romania, Hungary, and Bulgaria. It
is hardly necessary to remind our readers how
quickly the West was frozen out of all these regions.

In fact, lest we forget, the United States made
one last attempt to come to terms with the Soviet
Union when it invited Soviet and Soviet satellite
participation in the Marshall Plan.[1] The decision by Stalin to turn down this invitation is
well known, as is the irresistible Russian pressure on its satellites that forced them to do
likewise. Particularly illuminating is the case
of Czechoslovakia, which initially accepted the
invitation to participate and then was forced to
withdraw.

In the following years, however, it clearly became obvious to the Soviet Union that this

decision might have been a mistake. U.S. military might was still supreme. America's political leadership, under Presidents Truman and Eisenhower and their forceful secretaries of state, Acheson and Dulles, was clear and purposeful. The Soviet leadership—painfully bringing its country out of the devastation of war, and applying its well-known concept of examining the entire gamut of the co-relation of power before making decisions—found its role to be disadvantageous, and it therefore determined that it would find a way back to membership in the world club, both to benefit its own position and to prevent decisions taken by others that might be disadvantageous to the Soviet role. The Soviets thus had a positive and compelling incentive to activate their diplomacy and to enter into a more constructive dialogue with the United States and its partners. But in view of the still overwhelming political, economic, and military strengths of the Western Alliance and the strong and innovative leadership of American diplomacy, it became clear to the Soviet leaders that a price had to be paid, a kind of entrance fee into the club, if their plans were to bear fruit.

There was a great deal of logic in the decision, on both sides, that Austria constituted the ideal place where Eastern and Western interests might meet. The continued Soviet occupation of part of Austria, in the center of Europe, tended to destabilize Germany and Italy, or at least to project possible destabilization towards both countries. Soviet withdrawal from Austria was therefore clearly desirable from a Western point of view. At the same time, the Soviet influence in Austria had remained limited due to Austrian statesmanship, which preserved a unified Austrian government and administration in the face of numerous difficulties and Soviet intrigues, and due to both the United States and its partners

giving every indication that they would strongly support the Austrian government's resolve.
Hence, unless the Soviets wanted a confrontation with a still dominant U.S., their position
in Austria was not likely to improve. Therefore, a concession leading to a Soviet withdrawal from Austria was, from the Soviet point of
view, not an excessive price to pay in return
for the diplomatic advantages that they anticipated and, in fact, received.

As we all know, this decision was followed by
prolonged and hard negotiations. This is the
only way in which one can negotiate successfully
with the Soviets, but the eventual Soviet willingness to withdraw was a withdrawal from an area
that it did *not* dominate. There was no other
area in which the Soviet Union was willing to pay
a similar price. In all other areas in which
Soviet troops were present, their role was one
of predominance, which did not characterize the
situation in Austria.

It is, therefore, not surprising that the Soviet troop withdrawal from Austria constituted
a unique situation, the second and last such
withdrawal to date. (An earlier Soviet withdrawal had been forced by American pressure from
the northern Iranian province of Azerbaijan.)

It should be emphasized that the Soviet Union
was willing to accept the Austrian State Treaty,
not because it had softened or had become more
"peace-loving," but because it saw a definite
advantage to its long but persistent course towards the rectification of the international
imbalance, which at that time favored the West.

The subsequent period of détente was another
method of achieving the same end. As former
Secretary of Defense Brown stated succinctly,
though perhaps also ruefully, when he characterized the period and illusions of détente:
"When we built, the Soviets built. When we
stopped building, the Soviets built."[2]

Let us now turn to Afghanistan. Although there was no treaty of neutralization, Afghanistan was, for all practical purposes, a neutralized country until April 1978. The Afghans, although they had fiercely defended their independence for centuries, were quite realistic about the way to deal with major powers and to balance them against each other as far as possible. They played that great game quite successfully, interspersed with bloody wars, between imperial Russia and Britain—then in control of India. After Britain left India in 1947, America took Britain's place only in part. As my predecessors and I administered U.S. policy in that region, we wished to give Afghanistan sufficient aid to help it protect its independence, but we recognized that the Soviet Union had a legitimate interest in good and stable conditions at its southern border, just as we recognized the Afghan government's interest in maintaining good relations with the Soviet Union. Consequently, every Afghan government, royal or republican, was extremely careful never to undertake any action inside Afghanistan or in its foreign relations that would in the slightest way be frowned upon in Moscow.

During the Eisenhower/Dulles administration, Afghanistan broke this rule once by applying to the United States for military assistance. Secretary of State John Foster Dulles wisely, in my opinion, refused this request because he felt that the remote location of Afghanistan would necessitate a major American military buildup in that country if we were to assist it effectively, and this would unnecessarily heat up relations with the Soviet Union. In consequence, the then Prime Minister Prince Mohammed Daoud turned to the Soviet Union and, ever since 1959, all Afghanistan's military assistance and training has been given by Russia. Also, Soviet economic and technical assistance to Afghanistan was twice as large as that granted by the United States.

It would seem accurate, therefore, to characterize Afghanistan's de facto status in those
years as one of neutralization, with a tilt towards the Soviet Union. The latter accepted this
situation: For many years they could, of course,
have taken over Afghanistan—lock, stock, and bar-
rel—and would then have run into the difficulties
that they experience now; or they could have accepted some kind of balance, in which case the
choice for the balancing power was between China
and America. Clearly, the Soviet Union preferred
the Americans, as more likely to respect Soviet
interests than the Chinese.

Hence, it is possible to draw this parallel between Afghanistan and Austria: namely that the
de facto neutralization of Afghanistan, like the
legal one in Austria, antedated and prepared for
the practical exercise of détente. Unfortunate-
ly, the state of affairs was violently changed
by the Communist coup of April 27, 1978, in which
the Russians were deeply implicated and after
which they took immediate steps to expand their
direct participation at all levels of the Afghan
administration.

This is not the place to reflect at length
about the motives of the Soviet and Afghan Communist leaders in destroying a state of affairs
that was quite favorable to Soviet interests.
It is, however, important to underline strongly
that no even remotely imaginable Soviet interests were threatened by the royal or the Daoud
regimes. Nor is it possible to assert, as some
writers have done, that the Soviet Union was
concerned over the spread of Islamic fundamen-
talism in Iran and wanted to prevent similar
events in neighboring Afghanistan, for the simple
reason that in April 1978, the shah was still in
power in Teheran.

What is certain is that the unanimous interpretation of that event by the countries

neighboring Afghanistan—Pakistan on the one hand;
Iran, both under the shah and the ayatollah on
the other; as well as Saudi Arabia; the Gulf
states; and even radical Iraq—was that the 1978
coup in Kabul constituted a Soviet projection of
force and power directed primarily at the Middle
East and thus at the jugular vein of the Western
economy and defense. This should not be surprising. Soviet aspirations in that direction are
of long duration. One need not go back to the
alleged "Testament of Peter the Great" (the au-
thenticity of which has been contested by scholars), which spoke of Russian ambitions to reach
warm-water ports. Certainly authentic is the
note from then Soviet Foreign Minister Vyacheslav
Molotov to German Foreign Minister Joachim von
Ribbentrop, in 1940 stating that Soviet aspirations lay "south of Baku and Batum in the general
direction of the Persian Gulf."[3]

What the Russians had not taken into account
(although they should have), was the character
of the Afghans, who are a fiercely independent
and a deeply religious people. They do not like
Communists, whom they regard as infidels. They
do not like a highly centralized government that
tells them what to do, and most of all they do
not like Russians. That, together with the stupidity and incapacity of the Afghan Communist
government, led to such a deep alienation of
every segment of the Afghan population that in
a short time the entire Afghan countryside was
up in arms—literally so—against the Kabul Communist government. By the end of the spring of
1979, it had become clear that the Communist
government, then headed by Nur Mohammed Taraki
and actually dominated by Hafizullah Amin, could
not remain in power without external help. When
at the end of August a large Soviet military
mission headed by General Petrovsky, deputy minister of defense of the Soviet Union, arrived in

Afghanistan to review the situation, it was absolutely clear what their conclusions would have
to be: either to let the Communist government
fall by its own weight and incapacity or to take
over the country themselves. The world knows
which option the Soviets chose.

Once again, the Russians miscalculated. While
the impact of overwhelming Soviet forces had
quickly cowed resistance in Prague, Budapest,
and East Berlin, it only fanned the flames of
resistance in Afghanistan. The people there
have fought invaders for generations and are not
about to stop now. Fighting is an honorable and
proud occupation, and to fight the infidels is
particularly rewarding, because a faithful Mos-
lem who dies in a *Jihad*("holy war") is promised
immediate entry into paradise. Moreover, in a
country of very primitive conditions, life is
cheap and death comes easily.

Although the Russian invasion of Afghanistan
in December 1979 was merely the second and virtually inevitable sequel to the first incursion
in 1978, the world, including the government in
Washington, awoke to the implications of this
Soviet move only after the Russian soldiers had
crossed the Afghan border. The American reaction, while very belated, was nevertheless strong
and forceful, at least verbally so, and thus led
immediately to a rapid decline in Soviet-American
relations, conjuring up the vision of a renewal
of the cold war. I cannot take the time here to
discuss to what extent the cold war ever really
stopped, or whether détente was more than a psychological illusion for America. It must, however, be admitted that Western Europe did, or believed that it did, receive certain benefits from
détente: the increase in political and economic
relations between East and West Europe; a slight
ease in the relationship between East and West
Germany; and, of course, the understandable

feeling of people living on a potential battlefield that the danger of war was less imminent.

The Afghan invasion finally awakened America
and underscored our need to begin at long last
to close the growing defense gap between the USSR
and the U.S. But it created a shock wave in Europe and encouraged a desire to contain the crisis in U.S.-USSR relations over Afghanistan.

Understanding as I am of the European move towards some sort of neutralization of Afghanistan,
I must nevertheless underscore my conviction that
such a move is stillborn, ill-conceived, and po-
tentially dangerous. Afghanistan is not Austria.
The government in Kabul is not the Renner government or its successor, but a purely Communist
puppet regime. No Afghan of any note, no tribe,
no city, can conceivably tolerate the continuation of a Communist government, or even a government in which the Communists participate. If
neutralization means nothing more than a fig leaf
in order to legitimize the continuation of Communist control, it can have no practical viabili-
ty. If neutralization were to mean a guarantee
that a Communist government could remain in Kabul
after Soviet troops withdrew, then the reality
is that no such guarantee can be given, because
such a government would immediately be massacred
by the irate Afghans. Nor is any coalition government possible, because no politician, no public figure, no respectable person of any kind,
can afford the stigma of being associated in any
way with the Communists. The life expectancy of
such a person would be very short indeed. Nor
is it conceivable that any kind of international
force could be established in order to guarantee
the survival of a Communist Afghan government.
It would be fought the same way as the Russians
are being fought. What country would want to
lend its sons to such a disreputable enterprise?

No, the only neutralization of Afghanistan conceivable would be if and when the Soviet Union
feels that its enterprise there has become as
counterproductive as the U.S. came to realize
that its own role was in Vietnam. If at that
time, and that is a big *if*, the USSR were to
seek a smoke screen behind which its actual aban-
donment of the Communist regime in Afghanistan
and the withdrawal of its troops could be effected, then a form of neutralization could serve
that purpose. After all, it is the role of diplomacy to create formulas under which a country
that is in a bind can emerge in a face-saving
fashion. It follows from the above that it is
in the Western interest, if it wishes to hasten
such a moment, to make the Soviet invasion of
Afghanistan as costly as possible by giving dis-
creet, but well-placed assistance to the Afghan
freedom fighters.

If a true neutralization of Afghanistan is to
be achieved, it would really mean a return to the
pre-1973 situation in one form or another. Nothing could be more harmful now than to extend initiatives or suggestions to the Soviet government
that would only encourage it in the belief that
the West might be prepared to connive in some
kind of scheme permitting it to continue to enjoy
the fruits of its conquest. If any neutralization is to come about, it can happen only *after*
the Russians have reached the point where they
want such a solution, at which time the initiative has to come *from them* and not from the West.

To sum up then: Is the Austrian formula ap-
plicable to Afghanistan? The answer is clearly
no. The nature of the Austrian government at the
time of its neutralization, the participation of
the Western Allies in the occupation of Austria,
and the whole range of circumstances is totally
different in the two countries. The Austrian
case is unique and, alas, is likely to remain so
for a long time.

Notes

1. Molotov rejected the American invitation
to participate in the Marshall Plan on July 2,
1947. He had initially accepted an invitation
to attend the explanatory meeting in Paris with
British and French delegates, and he arrived in
Paris on June 27, 1947. As of June 28, Molotov
appeared to lean toward collaboration with the
West on economic recovery, but on July 2, he
felt compelled to break off the negotiations and
announced Soviet nonparticipation in the plan.

2. Secretary Harold Brown, The Salt II Treaty
Hearings before the Committee on Foreign Relations, U.S. Senate, 96th Congress, 1st session,
part 5. (Washington, D.C.: Government Printing
Office, 1979), p. 133.

3. Raymond James Sontag and James Stuart Bed-
die, eds., *Nazi-Soviet Relations, 1939-1941:
Documents from the Archives of the German Foreign
Office* (Washington, D.C.: U.S. Department of
State, 1948), pp. 258-59. The Molotov statement
regarding Soviet aspirations toward the Persian
Gulf was contained in the Soviet note to Germany
of November 25, 1940. Specifically, the Soviet
government indicated that it would be prepared
to accept the draft of the four-power pact, which
the Reich foreign minister had outlined in a
conversation of November 13, regarding political
collaboration and reciprocal economic support if
a number of conditions were met: among others,
"Provided that the area south of Batum and Baku
in the general direction of the Persian Gulf is
recognized as the center of the aspirations of
the Soviet Union." This was one of the stiff
conditions put by the Soviet government to the
German government as a price for Russia's ad-
herence to the pact, and it was the unaccepta-
bility of these conditions that clinched Hitler's decision to undertake the invasion of Russia.

FRITZ BOCK

Austrian Neutrality

The permanent neutrality under international law
that Austria has enjoyed since 1955 is an un-
precedented and unique phenomenon in the history
of Europe, both in its legal basis and in its
practical application. The following comments
are intended to prove that. I will not deal with
the various definitions of neutrality law—it will
be assumed that these are familiar—rather, I will
elaborate on the Austrian special case.

When Germany surrendered on May 8, 1945, Austria was occupied by the four Allied powers, and
the occupation zones, like those in Germany, were
defined territorially. The city of Vienna, which
is one of the nine federal states according to
the Austrian federal constitution, was also divided into four occupation zones. In addition,
the first district—the central city, which houses
all governmental centers—received a quadripartite
occupation, inasmuch as the four occupation
powers alternated command of that district month
by month. This was an essential difference from
the occupation arrangement in Berlin.

It was understandably Austria's goal to achieve
full freedom as quickly as possible through the
withdrawal of the occupation troops. To this end,
a *state treaty* between Austria and the Allied
powers was necessary—not a *peace treaty*. Between
1938 and 1945 Austria did not exist as a state,
so it could not have been at war and thus, a
peace agreement would have been inappropriate.

More than 350 rounds of negotiations were required to achieve this state treaty! But while
Austria had to recognize the reality of the

occupation during that time, it did not accept
the continuation of the occupation over the long
run. Even so, there are several reasons why ten
years had to pass before Austria attained its
goal—the reestablishment of full sovereignty.
Most of these reasons, but not all, can be found
in the Soviet Union's attitude. For a long time,
there were doubts in Washington about whether it
would be advisable to free Austria completely,
because there were fears that this might result
in strong Soviet influence there. Toward the
end of the forties, however, these fears were
eliminated through the intensive efforts of the
then ambassador to Washington, Karl Gruber. But
Austria did not yet have its freedom. Then, in
1954 at the state treaty negotiations in Berlin,
the Soviet Union offered to free Austria under the
condition that small, symbolic, military contin-
gents of the four Allies remain in the country.
Austria refused the offer. It was not until April
1955 that the Soviet Union was prepared to conduct final negotiations on completely ending the
occupation of Austria. These negotiations took
place in Moscow and resulted in the drafting of
a state treaty that was solemnly signed in Vienna on May 15, 1955.

To add a small but significant detail: This
draft still contained a formulation, agreed to
at Moscow, stating that Austria would be held ac-
countable for its "participation in the war." As
was already noted, Austria could not have participated in the war as a state. Still, this
passage was insisted upon. Former Federal Chancellor Leopold Figl finally managed to have this
passage stricken at the last round of negotiations on the final text of the treaty on May 14,
1955, in Vienna.

The question was then—and is now: What prompted
the Soviet Union to end the occupation of Austria?
Moscow's policy certainly was not determined by

Johann Strauss or the beautiful blue Danube or
other such considerations. But in 1955, a man
ruled in Moscow who understood the world as it
is; Nikita Khrushchev apparently knew that the
cold war could not result in Soviet gains. He
opened the Russian gate to the West in order to
make his country a trustworthy partner in international relations. We know that this has
changed again, but it was the case at that time.
Austria's release was a central part of Khrushchev's policy. We know that, even many years
later, the Austrian State Treaty has repeatedly
been cited by Moscow as proof of the Soviet
Union's new global policy.

Aside from these decisive Soviet considerations, Austria had to contribute to the attain-
ment of its complete freedom as well. This
contribution consisted of Austria's declaration
of permanent neutrality under international law.
Austria had never been a neutral state, but the
new situation virtually forced this international legal solution.

That Austria became a neutral state and that
all Austrians sincerely welcomed this solution
is based, inter alia, on Austria's geographical situation and her military potential. Beyond that, one should not forget that Austria,
Switzerland, and Liechtenstein form a barrier
of neutral territory in Europe. The existence
and effectiveness of this barrier is of major
importance to the political balance in Europe.
Austria has been striving to emphasize this importance through Vienna's becoming the third
seat—after New York and Geneva—of the United
Nations and other international organizations.
The large material sacrifices made by the Republic of Austria to this end—for example, the
erection of appropriate buildings known as
"U.N. City" in Vienna—were a contribution Austria gladly made.

Neutrality is not, as the Russians would have liked, a component part of the Austrian State Treaty. At the final negotiations in Moscow, the Austrian government's delegation only made a binding agreement that Austria would become permanently neutral at the moment the last foreign soldier left Austria. No, this is not a game of semantics! If neutrality were determined by the State Treaty, then the parties to the treaty would have the right to codetermine Austria's neutral policy. What that could have meant requires no elaboration. As matters stand, however, Austria decides its neutral policy alone. From this, one can already see that the development of Austrian neutrality was a unique process in European history. As far as the legal basis of Austria's permanent neutrality is concerned, one should keep in mind that the neutral status was made a component part of Austria's federal constitution and is therefore under a special, inner-Austrian legal guarantee. This is not true of, for example, Swedish neutrality. The Austrian parliament did not pass that constitutional amendment until October 26, 1955—the first day in more than seventeen years (March 11, 1938 to October 25, 1955) that there were no foreign soldiers in the country.

As far as the practical implementation of Austrian neutrality is concerned, it is not only different from Swedish neutrality, as has already been mentioned, it also differs considerably from Swiss neutrality. According to the Austrian interpretation, neutrality includes, for example, Austria's obligation to refrain from interfering in the internal politics of other nations. This is a clear difference from Swedish neutrality as it was implemented until the end of the period of Socialist government in Sweden; Sweden never hesitated to take very definite stands on events in other countries. The

difference between Swiss and Austrian neutrality
consists in Austria's pursuit of a so-called active neutrality, while Swiss neutrality can be
considered an absence of policy. Austria's membership in the United Nations is a significant
example of this difference. So far, Switzerland
has declined membership; there is a valid constitutional basis for this. According to generally acknowledged norms of international law, a
neutral state cannot join any international organizations that are supranational in nature and
can therefore make decisions that members are
obliged to accept. According to international
law, a neutral state would run the risk of being
bound to resolutions that contradict its neutrality. Austria subscribes to that position only to
a limited degree: as for example, with the policy
of integration. But at the state treaty negotiations in Moscow, Austria had already stipulated
her future membership in the United Nations, thus
submitting to the supranational decisions of the
Security Council. This intent was welcomed unanimously by the Allied powers at the time. In contrast to Switzerland's interpretation of neutral
policy, Austria has consistently offered her good
offices in international affairs. That an Austrian was secretary-general of the United Nations
for almost ten years and that the secretary-
general of the Council of Europe is the second
Austrian to hold that post, are results of this
active neutrality.

This system of active neutrality is also a consequence of Austria's geographical situation.
Since Austria lies on the edge of the demarcation
line of international politics, East-West contacts in, with, and across Austria are necessarily livelier than those of other Western European
countries. Austria's centuries-old history also
plays a corresponding role. One must not forget
that Vienna was the main seat of the Roman-German

emperor for over 500 years. For the rest of its
past, that strange and unique historical European structure Austria-Hungary was a monarchy
under whose crown twelve nations lived next to
and with each other. German-speaking Austrians,
Magyars (Hungarians), Czechs and Slovaks, Slovenes and Serbs, Ukrainians, Muhammadan Monte-
negrins, etc., formed a mixture of nationalities
within the borders of a single empire—the only
one of its kind in European history. Travelers
in all of these countries still encounter evidence of and witnesses to this past, and Austrian visitors are still approached on the subject
of that past—not only by older people in these
nations, but also by young people. The result
of all of this is that the Austrian of today has
a far better knowledge and understanding of what
is taking place in that wide geographical area,
despite all the diametrical differences in sociopolitical approaches. The Austrian knows the
mentality of the peoples he lived with for centuries better than other Europeans do, and can
therefore offer some good advice. It is almost
natural that this also affects the economic
sphere. Many international transactions take
place in or through Austria for that very reason and stimulate the Austrian economy. Because
of that, Vienna is also the preferred seat of
numerous semiofficial and private international
associations that offer their services to the
makers of official policy in the economic as
well as the political sphere. An example is the
Donaueuropaeisches Institut (Organization for
International Economic Relations).

One thing must be remembered: Austrian neutrality is a matter of international law. It is
not a sociopolitical issue. In other words, it
must not be confused with nonalignment or neutralism. *Nonalignment* generally refers to those
countries that, while they do not belong to any

political grouping of nations, do support the
policies of one group or another in individual
cases. Neutralism, on the other hand, can be
called a system without a clear and definite
political line. Austria, however, is a full-
fledged member of the Western system of political democracy. That is not only an obvious
necessity for historical reasons, it is also,
in its way, a fundamental advantage. The West
can be confident that the Western democratic
system is prevailing in Austria, unshakably and
without restriction, and will continue to do so;
the East knows and recognizes this. The East
has therefore never attempted to exert pressure
on Austria regarding this orientation. If such
an attempt were ever made, it would face ada-
mant Austrian resistance.

HANSPETER NEUHOLD

Permanent Neutrality
and Nonalignment
Similarities and Differences

Introduction

The sixth summit conference of the nonaligned
states held at Havana in September 1979 provides
an appropriate opportunity for comparing the
legal status of permanent neutrality and the
political doctrine of nonalignment. Not only
the general public but even experts on foreign
affairs in permanently neutral states are rather
ill-informed about the characteristics of the
nonaligned movement. Similarly, the status of
permanent neutrality is often not correctly per-
ceived in the nonaligned camp. Therefore, an
effort at filling in the information gaps and
dispelling misunderstandings on both sides seems
to be worthwhile.

The first part of this article will consist of
brief summaries of the main features of permanent neutrality and nonalignment; a comparison
of their most striking similarities and differences will then be made. This paper is based
on legal and diplomatic documents, "tradition-
alist" scholarly literature, and a recent empirical study.[1] One important finding of the following comparative analysis should be stated at the
outset: Both the aspects that the permanently
neutral and the nonaligned states obviously appear to have in common and those that clearly
separate them from each other at first sight

will have to be qualified against the background
of the actual behavior of the countries concerned, so that the final picture that will
emerge as a result of this article is going to
be more complex than might be expected.

Permanent Neutrality

A permanently neutral state[2] is, by virtue of
an international treaty or a binding unilateral
declaration, under a legal obligation not to participate in any future war. Hence, it has to
observe the norms of the law of neutrality whenever a war as defined by international law breaks
out. These obligations, which are partly codi-
fied in international treaties[3] and partly based
on customary law, can be divided into four categories:

1. the obligations of abstention can best be
    summed up as the (absolute[4]) prohibition of
    direct or indirect provision of military sup-
    port to belligerents. Consequently, a neu-
    tral state must not, for instance, furnish
    troops or war material to belligerent par-
    ties, nor may it grant loans for military
    purposes to them.

2. Under the obligations of prevention, neutrals
    are not to permit states involved in a war to
    engage in military activities on their terri-
    tories, e.g., the establishment of military
    bases. Similarly, the transit of belligerent
    troops or the overflight of military air-
    craft must be impeded. Under the Damocles'
    sword of self-help, compliance with these
    obligations lies in the neutral's own nation-
    al interest. For should the neutral state
    prove, at least over a certain period of time,
    unable or unwilling to put an end to such en-
    croachments on its neutrality, the belligerent

negatively affected by them is entitled to do
so itself. This would mean, however, that
armed hostilities between the belligerent
parties would spread to the neutral state's
territory, so that it would be drawn into
the war—the very result that it wanted first
and foremost to avoid by choosing a neutral
position!

3. The principle of impartiality imposes upon
    neutral states the obligation of treating
    belligerent states on an equal footing in
    all those nonmilitary sectors where no ob-
    ligations of abstention exist. If, for in-
    stance, a neutral decides to place an embar-
    go on an agricultural product, it must apply
    the embargo equally to all warring parties.[5]

4. Finally, by virtue of the obligations of
    tolerance, the neutral state must put up with
    certain acts by belligerents that in peace-
    time would be clearly illegal. In particu-
    lar, it has to submit to restrictions on the
    freedom of the high seas, because blockades
    and the seizure of neutral merchantmen carry-
    ing contraband are permissible in naval war-
    fare.

These norms of the law of temporary neutrality
have to be borne in mind if one wants to really
understand the obligations that permanently neutral states must fulfill even in peacetime. In
short, such states have to refrain from any act
that would make it impossible or very difficult
for them to abide by the above obligations; they
must do everything to be able to comply with them
if and when war breaks out between other states.
According to the 1954 "Official Neutrality Conception" of Switzerland, primary and secondary
obligations can be distinguished in this respect:[6]

——It goes without saying that a permanently neutral state must not launch a war of aggression—not only is this the act par excellence
of abandoning neutrality, but it is also contrary to a prohibition binding on all states
by virtue of a norm of universal international
law.

——In addition, states that are subject to the
status of permanent neutrality must maintain
their independence, territorial integrity,
and neutrality and must provide for their own
armed defense in advance, even if only to live
up to their obligations of prevention in future wars. The minimum that their prepara-
tions have to attain is determined by the international standard, i.e., the average defensive efforts undertaken by comparable countries.[7] Despite certain shortcomings, the
proportion of GNP spent on defense by the
states concerned can be used as a yardstick
to measure the criterion of the international
standard.[8]

——As for the secondary obligations, the general
formula mentioned above has far-reaching implications especially for the security policy
and the international economic relations of
permanently neutral states.

When it comes to providing for its defense, a
permanently neutral state must rely primarily on
its own strength, because membership in a military alliance, even for purely defensive purposes, is ruled out by its special status; other-
wise it would be confronting an insoluble dilemma
whenever one of its allies is attacked by an aggressor and becomes involved in a war. On the
one hand, if a permanently neutral state took up
arms to come to the victim's rescue in accordance
with the alliance treaty, it would violate the

obligations of abstention and impartiality. If,
on the other hand, it were to invoke these principles resulting from its neutrality, it would,
of course, refuse to abide by its main obligation
as an ally. In order to forestall the emergence
of this dilemma, permanently neutral states are
barred from entering into alliance agreements
altogether, even with other countries endowed
with this status.

Similarly, they must not permit the establishment of foreign military bases on their territories. For when the owner of such bases becomes
involved in a war, their use constitutes a breach
of the obligations of abstention and may draw the
neutral state into the war.

Although permanent neutrality thus casts a long
shadow on the security policy of the states that
have adopted this status, it prohibits neither
"unilateral alliances," i.e., the guaranty of the
neutral's independence and territorial integrity
against aggression by other states nor ad hoc re-
quests for help by neutrals if they are attacked
and their neutrality is thus terminated. Moreover, although permanent neutrality and participation in a system of collective security appear
mutually exclusive in principle, the flexibility
of the UN system allows permanently neutral
states also to apply for admission to that organization.[9] The UN Charter does not call for
automatic sanctions by its members against the
guilty states whenever an act of aggression, a
breach of the peace, or a threat to the peace
occur. The Security Council must decide in each
concrete case whether such a situation requiring
forcible measures exists, against whom they are
to be taken, whether armed force is to be re-
sorted to or nonmilitary sanctions suffice, and
finally whether all member states or only some
of them are to participate in those enforcement
measures. In point of fact, Article 48 of the

charter expressly authorizes the council to call upon some members only when it deems action necessary to maintain or restore international peace and security. Permanently neutral member states can thus be exempted from military sanctions that would jeopardize their status.[10]

In a similar vein, permanently neutral states must refrain from economic ties that, because of the scope of the areas envisaged for cooperation and/or the institutional integration, are so close as to compromise the future observance of the law of neutrality. For these reasons Austria, Sweden, and Switzerland were free to become full-fledged members of the European Free Trade Association (EFTA) but not of the European Communities. In the latter case, they had to settle for special free-trade arrangements in 1972 that contained additional provisions to safeguard the special position of the three European neutral states.

Last but not least, permanent neutrality entails the obligation to practice a policy of neutrality. The objective of this policy is to strengthen this status in the eyes of the other states beyond compliance with the legal obligations. Whereas in the aforementioned area governed by international law, cognitive expectations concerning specific behavior patterns have hardened into normative ones,[11] the concrete steps to be taken in the pursuit of the policy of neutrality are not determined by international law. They are instead left to the discretion of each government concerned. Yet ultimately the success of this policy[12] depends on the response of the rest of international society to it. What may appear to be a paradox becomes clear once the goals to be reached are taken into account.

The component of the "positive" policy of neutrality is to render the permanently neutral

countries' special international status more attractive to other states. All too often, neutrals have been accused of idly sitting by during international conflicts—letting the belligerents pull the chestnuts out of the fire for
them too. Hence, they have to convince their
critics that they can assume certain functions
that are useful to others. For instance, permanently neutral states are particularly qualified to offer their good offices or mediation in
international conflicts, to contribute contin-
gents to peacekeeping operations, or to invite
international organizations to set up their headquarters and to host international conferences
on their territories.[13]

The "negative" element of the policy of neutrality is to enhance the credibility of a permanently neutral state's capability and determination
to effectively defend itself if necessary. The
"entrance and occupation price" strategy developed by neutrals as a variation on the theme of
deterrence aims at demonstrating to a would-be
aggressor that the costs of attempting to in-
vade and occupy their territory in terms of human
casualties, the loss of war material, and political good-will, as well as time, will outweigh
the advantages derived from occupation.[14]

A final point that is worth mentioning in the
context of this paper concerns the ideological
dimension of permanent neutrality. States that
have opted for this status are not required to
remain ideologically neutral. Yet their governments and media in particular undermine the
credibility of their country's neutrality if,
when taking sides, they do not at least moderate
the tone of their criticism.

At present, only the permanent neutrality of
Austria and Switzerland does not give rise to
any doubts. Switzerland had actually maintained
this status ever since her expansionist ambitions

were thwarted at the battles of Marignano and
Pavia early in the sixteenth century. Her permanent neutrality was eventually recognized and
guaranteed by the then great powers in the course
of the comprehensive political settlement after
the defeat of Napoleon in 1815. Austria benefited from a brief thaw in the cold war as the
Soviet Union agreed to join the three other occupation powers, France, the United Kingdom, and
the U.S., in restoring Austrian independence by
affixing her signature to the Austrian State
Treaty and ratifying it; in exchange, Austria
declared her permanent neutrality in 1955.[15]

Sweden has been observing permanent neutrality
as a principle of her foreign policy ever since
the early nineteenth century, but without having
entered into any legal obligation to this effect.
Finland's status can at best be described as
asymmetrical neutrality, with a pro-Soviet bias.
The peculiar legal foundation of this status is
the 1948 Treaty of Friendship, Co-operation, and
Mutual Assistance, which was renewed in 1955 and
1970.[16] Whether Laos can really be included
among the permanently neutral states as a result
of her Declaration of Neutrality and the corresponding multilateral Geneva agreements of 1962
is open to question, especially in the light of
more recent events.[17] Finally, a good case can
be made for the Vatican state's permanent neutrality under one of the three Lateran Treaties
concluded between Italy and the Holy See in 1929;
yet because of its size and other peculiarities,
it can be omitted for the purposes of the present
analysis.[18]

Nonalignment

In the brief history of the nonalignment movement,[19] three phases can be distinguished that
highlight the evolution of its main features.

The first period, which lasted from the mid-1950s to the mid-1960s, was characterized by the struggle for self-assertion and noninvolvement in the cold war on the one hand and by efforts to strengthen the nonaligned camp by accelerating the decolonization process on the other.

Thus, the key concept of nonalignment was construed rather strictly: Membership in military alliances and the leasing of military bases to foreign powers,[20] at least in the "context of Great Power Conflicts,"[21] were denounced as contrary to the principles of the emerging movement. The nonaligned states also rejected the establishment of an alliance among themselves and did not regard themselves as a third bloc in world affairs. They solely envisioned loose cooperation within the nonaligned group and declared themselves in favor of strengthening the UN.

On the legal plane, they stressed *panch shila*, the five principles of "peaceful coexistence." These principles were laid down for the first time in the preamble of a trade and communication agreement concerning Tibet concluded between India and the People's Republic of China in 1954.[22] In general, respect for territorial integrity and sovereignty, nonaggression, noninterference in internal affairs, equality and mutual benefit, and peaceful coexistence are well-established norms of international law, with the exception of the last, very vague and ill-defined, principle.[23] It is also hardly surprising that the nonaligned countries singled out principles that particularly protect the weaker states in the international arena.

Especially during this first phase, spokesmen of the nonaligned group underlined the moral superiority of their approach to world affairs. In doing so, they tried to counter those critics who, like John Foster Dulles, branded their

stance as immoral.[24] By refusing to see, in
principle, the cold war as a struggle between
good and evil, they also tried to create an additional positive, superior mission for their
group. Insisting on their right to judge each
specific dispute between East and West on its
merits, they emphasized the active role of nonalignment. States espousing this doctrine were
thus to contribute to international peace by
offering their good offices and mediation to
the "cold war" protagonists and even by acting
as arbitrators between them. Their search for
identity as a separate factor in the international system was further facilitated by the
awareness of their common (Afro-Asian) cultural
similarities.

Their common low level of economic development
also helped in this respect, although economic
demands were played down during the first dec-
ade. Thus, merely three-and-a-half of the
twenty-seven points of the declaration adopted
at the first Conference of Heads of State of
Government of the Non-Aligned Countries held in
Belgrade in 1961[25] dealt with economic matters,
and only one of the eleven chapters of the Programme of the second summit which took place in
Cairo in 1964, was devoted to them.[26]

Throughout those years, emphasis was placed
instead on speeding up the accession to independence by colonial territories. The nonaligned states very skillfully used the UN to
this end. They transformed the right of peoples to self-determination enshrined, in general terms, in the UN Charter into a superior
fundamental norm in the Kelsenian sense. Their
definition of the people entitled to self-
determination as the population living within
the boundaries drawn—however arbitrarily—by the
former colonial powers of dependent overseas
territories[27] left within the Third World,

especially the African states, the seeds of future ethnic and tribal conflicts.[28]
    The second half of the 1960s witnessed a peri-
od of decline and disappointment for the nonaligned group. Its strength did not live up to
the hopes and expectations of its founders, for
a number of reasons. Cohesion between the more
radical and the moderate member countries proved
to be precarious. The rapprochement between the
two superpowers in the wake of the Cuban missile
crisis made the strategy of playing them off
against each other more difficult. In addition
to this "Big Twoism," events in the Congo and
U.S. involvement in the Dominican Republic and in
Vietnam demonstrated the weakness of the Third
World countries against the military clout of
great powers. Furthermore, with the passage of
time, the psychological fascination of the policies originally hailed as an alternative to traditional power politics[29] was bound to wane,
especially as several founding fathers of the
nonaligned group, such as Presidents Ben Bella,
Nkrumah, and Sukarno, were ousted by military
coups during those years.
    It was therefore all the more surprising that
instead of gradually disappearing from the international scene as a group, the nonaligned states
recovered and came to life again in the 1970s.
    Not only did their number keep growing, but the
movement increasingly spread to Latin America.[30]
Whereas the Belgrade and the Cairo conferences
of 1961 and 1964 were attended by twenty-five and
forty-seven states respectively, the number of
full-fledged participants rose to fifty-four at
the 1970 Lusaka Summit, to seventy-five at the
1973 Algiers Summit, and eventually to eighty-
six at the 1976 Colombo Summit.
    Still more importantly, the emphasis of the non-
aligned program has been shifted to demands for
economic reforms. The Third World has come to

realize that political and legal decolonization
have not solved its problems, because their
genuine independence requires economic decolonization as well. It has dawned upon developing
countries that the neoliberal international economic system established after the Second World
War served only the recovery and development of
the (Western) industrialized states, whereas the
promised trickle-down effect, permitting the
Third World to automatically obtain a fair share
of the benefits, did not materialize. On the
contrary, the gap between rich and poor countries keeps widening. It is no wonder that the
latter are focusing their demands on the creation of the New International Economic Order
based on the principles of equality and justice.
This new order is not restricted to a few cos-
metic operations within the existing system. It
is conceived as a comprehensive scheme of fundamental structural changes that are to eliminate
the present asymmetries in international economic relations. In particular, the developing
countries insist on ending their subservient role
as suppliers of raw materials, confronting terms
of trade that are continuously deteriorating. The
New International Economic Order also includes
far-reaching reforms in such areas as international monetary matters, development aid, foreign
investments, technology transfer, and industriali-
zation.[31] The nonaligned camp espoused those demands in declarations adopted at their last three
summit conferences in Lusaka (1970), Algiers
(1973), and Colombo (1976). It has become the
political spearhead of the "Group of 77"—which
can, to a certain extent, be compared with a
trade union of global dimensions.
    The common economic plight of the nonaligned
countries has so far prevented the disintegration of the movement that could have resulted
from increased membership and heterogeneity and

from the shift from bipolar East-West confrontation to multipolarity in the international system.[32]

On the contrary, the nonaligned movement has
strengthened its hand in this worldwide, mainly
socioeconomic, struggle by recently enhancing its
institutional cohesion.[33] Thus, conferences at
the levels of heads of state or government as well
as of foreign ministers not only are convened more
frequently and more regularly but have also undergone a change in character. Previously, nonaligned summits were held as rather informal
meetings of like-minded political leaders who
discussed mainly political issues. In the seventies, these high-level conferences have become
more structured and are more carefully prepared.
Economic problems are debated on a footing at
least equal to that of political items on the
agenda. Lengthy documents are published at the
conclusion of these meetings.

Moreover, it was decided at the 1970 Lusaka
Conference to appoint the summit chairperson
(i.e., the head of state or government of the
respective host country), coordinator and official spokesman of the movement for the three-
year period until the following meeting at the
highest level was held. In addition, at the
third summit, held in Algiers in 1973, the nonaligned states established a Coordination Bureau
whose membership was increased from fifteen to
twenty-five at the Colombo conference, and to
thirty-six at the Havana Summit. It operates at
the levels of the states' foreign ministers and
ambassadors to the UN. As its name indicates,
the bureau is charged with coordinating nonaligned activities during the intervals between
summit conferences; its terms of reference also
include the supervision of the implementation
of decisions and the discussion of urgent international problems (especially crises), as

well as the submission of proposals for their settlement.

Small groups of between two and seventeen countries coordinate and control the actual implementation of nonaligned action programs. The number of these coordinating groups was increased to fifteen at the Colombo Summit in 1976 and to eighteen at the Havana Conference in 1979. The sectors they cover range from trade and monetary matters to tourism and sports. In addition, groups of experts and working groups are set up for specific purposes if need be. Another step in the direction of institutionalization was the creation, in 1976, of a pool of nonaligned news agencies. This attempt at decolonizing information is to break the domination of the "Northern" news agencies, the transnational corporations in the field, which are criticized for providing coverage of the Third World that is too little and biased. What has not yet been accomplished—for fear of dangerously strengthening the hand of the country that it hosts—is the creation of a permanent secretariat of the nonaligned movement.[34]

Similarities and Differences

Nonmembership in military alliances
The most obvious common denominator of permanent neutrality and nonalignment consists of nonparticipation in military alliances, even among permanently neutral or nonaligned states themselves. With respect to permanent neutrality, there exists a clear-cut legal prohibition to this effect; the refusal of nonaligned countries to enter into military arrangements is based solely on a political maxim.

Moreover, this nonparticipation has been restricted, from the very beginning, to multilateral military alliances and other agreements "concluded in the context of Great Power

conflicts,"[35] which were not defined, however.
As already mentioned, the very *raison d'être* for
the emergence of the nonaligned group was its
desire to steer clear of involvement in the cold
war, a conflict between industrialized powers
that was of only secondary concern to them. Consequently, membership in NATO, the Warsaw Pact,
CENTO, or SEATO was regarded as out of the question for a nonaligned state. Yet OAS did not
fall into the category of unacceptable alliances;
for Cuba was one of the founding members of the
movement, which in recent years has been joined
by several other Latin American States too. The
same seems also to apply, for instance, to both
the multilateral military arrangement entered into by France with the Defense Council of Equato-
rial Africa and the bilateral military treaties
concluded by the United Kingdom with ten states,
all of whom were admitted to nonaligned conferences.[36] Obviously, all these arrangements were
excluded from "the context of Great Power conflicts"—a debatable decision, especially in the
light of increasing East-West rivalry in Africa
in recent years.

Despite the aforementioned recent progress in
the creation of an institutional network, the
present degree of institutionalization within
the nonaligned group would still appear compati-
ble with its refusal to form a third bloc in
world affairs.[37] This diagnosis is borne out by
the only partial cohesion in its voting record
in the UN General Assembly. For whereas the
nonaligned countries close their ranks whenever
economic and decolonization issues are put to
the vote, they are divided on other political
problems, especially those concerning East-West
relations. It is a fine point as to when their
integration would reach an intensity contrary
to the above principle. It may become relevant
if and when the developing countries do embark

on the strategy of collective self-reliance that they have been verbally stressing ever since the 1970 Lusaka Conference. If taken seriously, closer economic cooperation—for instance through the creation of a common market—may necessitate restrictions on the sovereignty of the states involved.

As to the permanently neutral states, their cooperation remains rather loose,[38] the friendly and cordial character of their mutual relations and their many common interests notwithstanding.

The factual differences between permanently neutral and nonaligned states

In regard to the following aspects, the differences between permanent neutrality and nonalignment seem to prevail—at least at first glance.

First and foremost, there is little if anything that permanently neutral and nonaligned states have in common in terms of their respective objective conditions. The permanently neutral states are all industrialized countries in Europe that stick to a Western, pluralist-democratic political system and to a (more or less) "capitalist" market-oriented economic order. Almost all nonaligned countries are situated in Africa, Asia, and South America. They share a low level of economic development. Many of them opted for a one-party political system and a Socialist planned economy.[39] If measured in terms of modern military hardware, GNP, or similar criteria, their power potential still appears negligible. Because they are small, albeit developed, however, the European neutrals are facing a number of economic problems familiar to developing countries.[40] Their exports are, in fact, concentrated on relatively few commodities and in few markets. To make matters worse, the structure of their foreign trade is also

unfavorable: Nonmanufactured goods account for
a higher share of their exports and manufactured
products, especially those requiring advanced
technology, a greater proportion of their im-
ports than in the international commercial relations of their larger counterparts. Their balance of trade tends to be negative. As compared
with the great powers in the economic field,
their primary sector is relatively more important, and the manufacturing sector is smaller
and restricted to only a few branches that can
compete in international markets. They are also lagging behind at the technological level.
The three countries in question are not affected
by these negative trends to the same degree:
Austria is worse off in the above respects than
Sweden and Switzerland. To make matters still
worse for all of them, in contradistinction to
other small developed countries, permanently
neutral states are barred from remedying these
structural weaknesses by embarking on economic
integration with other countries and thus creating larger economic units beyond certain rather
low thresholds.

Of course, that is not to say that the permanently neutral states are sitting in the same
economic boat as the Third World. What their
governments and populations should realize,
however, is that their interests need not always be identical to those of the leading industrial powers.

Other recent developments have further nar-
rowed the gap between developed and developing
states. Changes in the weight of the various
power factors have strengthened the position
of the developing countries in the international arena.[41]

On the one hand, despite tremendous "progress"
in the destructive capabilities of modern weapons, the value of the developed states' military

potential declined in the age of the balance of
(nuclear) terror and the danger of conventional
warfare between nuclear powers and their allies
escalating across the nuclear threshold. Similarly, high standards of technological development and managerial know-how do not automatically provide the keys to superpower status, as is
demonstrated by the case of Japan.

On the other hand, the value of the military
instruments of the developing countries is not
on the wane. At least "primitive" nuclear weapons are within the reach of a growing number of
them. Moreover, the threat of resorting to them
by a developing country—its back against the
wall because of misery and famine—must appear
credible and thus becomes relevant in the wield-
ing of power. The conventional arsenals of
quite a few Third World countries make at least
traditional gunboat diplomacy impossible. These
arsenals should deter the dispatch of expedi-
tionary corps—for example, to secure access to
natural resources. Finally, the Vietnam conflict convincingly demonstrated that by applying guerrilla strategy, "military have-nots"
can even resist a nuclear superpower, if the
latter proves unable to adjust to this type of
warfare and has to fight on unfamiliar terrain.

The success of the oil weapon in 1973/74 drove
home the lesson of the increasing strength to be
drawn from the possession of raw materials vital
to modern industry.[42] This is true even if the
countries concerned still need foreign assistance for the prospecting, extraction, process-
ing, and marketing of the natural resources in
question, provided they join forces and are
relatively invulnerable to counterpressure.
Public opinion, which the Third World has learned
to use to its advantage through the UN and other-
wise, is also becoming less of a *quantité négli-
geable* in world affairs. Finally, the chaos

power of the South keeps growing, as the global
problems of mankind—be it nuclear proliferation,
energy, or pollution—cannot be solved without
its cooperation. All this does not mean that
all of a sudden the tables are turned in the developing states' favor, but merely that they are
no longer helpless underdogs in international
power politics.

The two types of states pursuing different kinds
of neutrality in a political sense are also dis-
tinguishable from a simple numerical point of
view. Up to now, permanent neutrality has been a
rather unusual status open to very few states.
For the countries in question were and are situated on the main front of great-power confrontation; at the same time, they benefited and will
continue to benefit from a privileged geopoliti-
cal position of secondary importance. The result was that the great powers jointly renounced
direct control over the territory of the state
whose permanent neutrality they therefore accepted.[43] This applies to Switzerland's primary
strategic trump card, the passes across the Alps,
as well as to the transformation in 1955 of Austria into a permanently neutral wedge in central
Europe that, together with Switzerland, extends
over a length of some 800 kilometers (and obviously favors the Warsaw Pact to the detriment
of NATO,[44] so that the USSR's decision to relin-
quish the eastern part of Austria in 1955 can be
understood. Similarly, Sweden's factual permanent neutrality today makes sense against the
background of the precarious Nordic Balance, with
Denmark and Norway having thrown in their lot
with NATO[45] and Finland trying to steer an independent course as a Western country in terms of
her political and economic structures, without
really antagonizing her powerful Soviet neighbor.

In contrast to the exceptional status of permanent neutrality that evolved in the era of the

European balance-of-power system, the majority
of the members of the contemporary society of
states has opted for its much more recent counterpart, which is the Third World's response to
the bipolar global system emerging after the
Second World War. Its success was facilitated
by the revolutionary advent of the nuclear age,
in which even the superpowers face annihilation
in a conflict fought with nuclear weapons by both
sides, and by the resulting shift to "milieu
goals,"—i.e., power politics through indirect
control and penetration instead of through territorial gains.[46] The great powers came therefore
to accept the refusal by the countries in the
"gray area" in the southern half of the globe to
take sides in their confrontation, the cold war,
and its successor, détente.

Legal status v. political doctrine
   Permanent neutrality is a legal status consisting of well-defined rights and obligations that
the state bound to it is not free to unilaterally
alter or terminate at will. By contrast, the
principles of nonalignment are not legally binding on the states subscribing to them: They
amount solely to a political doctrine from which
deviation is permissible. However, the normal
behavior patterns of nonaligned states could also harden into normative rules if they are consistently practiced during a sufficient period
of time and with *opinio iuris*.[47] Should these
two prerequisites be met, the principles of nonalignment would be transformed into norms of
customary international law. This evolution has
not yet occurred. One would be hard put especially to prove the existence of *opinio iuris*;
but such a development is by no means impossible.
For the time being, however, the advantages resulting from the flexibility of merely political
maxims seem to outweigh, in the eyes of the

nonaligned states, those stemming from the pre-
dictability of their behavior for other countries
should those principles become legally binding.

"Passive" permanent neutrality
v. "active" nonalignment

One widespread misunderstanding concerns the
political role and the ideological dimension of
both permanent neutrality and nonalignment. On
the one hand, representatives of nonaligned countries are among the most outspoken critics of the
allegedly passive, isolationist stance of permanently neutral states in world affairs.[48] On the
other hand, both foreign policy experts and public opinion in the West, and also in permanently
neutral states, accuse the nonaligned group of
"immoral neutralism" because it refuses to support what these critics regard as the just cause
in the central East-West confrontation.

On closer analysis, both reproaches turn out
to be rather ill-founded. As mentioned earlier,
permanently neutral states pursue a "positive"
policy of neutrality, whose active character cannot be denied. By trying to contribute to the
peaceful settlement of international conflicts
in various ways—such as offering their good offices and mediation, acting as protecting powers,
hosting international conferences and international organizations, or participating in peacekeeping operations—they too engage in the bridgemanship upon which some nonaligned leaders prided
themselves.[49] They are well aware that their
survival as neutrals depends, to a large extent,
on the success of their attempts to make themselves useful to other states. Realistically
taking account of their small number and the
limitations upon their power, they prefer, however, the channels of quiet diplomacy, so that
their activities sometimes may not receive the
publicity that they would deserve.

At any rate, the criticism of the neutrals'
passive stance in world affairs was at best justified in that past age when the right to go to war
at will was considered an element of state sovereignty, but the negative effects of armed hostilities were limited by the (relatively) "primitive"
weapons technology and the mechanisms of the European balance-of-power system.[50] Neutrals were
regarded as seconds in a permissible duel between
other states.[51] By their mere noninvolvement
therein they rendered, in this traditional view,
a positive service, which helped to isolate the
belligerents and facilitated their return to peace.
In the contemporary era of nuclear overkill capabilities, in which the use of force is outlawed,
and in an increasingly interdependent world, permanently neutral states are not blind to these
realities. They realize full well that they too
are required to make those active contributions
to the solution of global problems for which they
are particularly qualified.

With regard to the ideological dimension of permanent neutrality, the states concerned, above
all Switzerland, did not remain passive on this
front either. In order to enhance their internal
cohesion, and to add to the legitimacy of their
status in the eyes of the rest of the world, the
permanently neutral states sought instead to create a national mission.[52] This mission was sometimes even propagated in universalist terms.
Thus, the Swiss time and again called for the
"Helvetization" of the world; if the other states
would only adopt their democratic, federalist,
and humanitarian ideals, eternal peace would
reign on earth....[53]

Those who denounce the "immoral" character of
nonalignment approach the East-West conflict as
a confrontation between good and evil. From this
point of view, those who are not for us are—indeed—against us. These critics fail to understand

that to the nonaligned states the cold war appeared in a different light. It was a conflict between their "natural" opponents, namely, blocs of industrialized countries. They therefore refused to take sides once and for all; such a step would only have compromised their newly won independence, and imposed military burdens on them; moreover, it could have drawn them into a fatal clash between the superpowers. Their attitude was thus dictated by their national interest—a principle that the opponents of "neutralism" would never question in the case of their own states.

That the nonaligned countries more strongly underscore the ideological superiority of their movement than the permanently neutral states do is hardly surprising. The moralistic undertones stem from their efforts to silence their critics and from their search for identity on the international scene as well as from self-confidence built on achievements and numerical strength.[54]

Another alleged difference is worth mentioning in this context. Nonaligned activism in the UN is sometimes quoted as evidence of a dynamic role played by these countries in world affairs,[55] which, in their view, the permanently neutral states are unable to share. True enough, the nonaligned states have gained control of those UN organs in which their voting power tips the scales. Yet the permanently neutral states do not sit idly by either.

Admittedly, Switzerland, because of her negative experiences as a member of the League of Nations, has not yet applied for admission to the UN. Austria, however—as a newcomer on the international scene in 1955—staked her hopes on the organization from the very beginning. And it cannot be denied that Sweden is among the most active members of the UN, one whose influence far exceeds her material power base.

After all, an Austrian citizen served almost
ten years as secretary-general of the organization. He had only three predecessors, and one
was a Swede. Vienna's most ambitious architec-
tural venture after the Second World War, the
"UN City," hosts IAEA, UNIDO, and other UN organs
and is to serve as an international conference
center. Sweden and Austria are second to none
when it comes to participating in UN peacekeeping.
    The above considerations are not to deny the
differences in the approaches to world affairs
adopted by the two groups of states. The European neutrals—whose time-honored, narrowly defined status is, in the main, restricted to legal
obligations in the military sector—emphasize
stability and the maintenance of a balance of
forces in international relations. Although the
nonaligned states also oppose shifts in the existing power structure leading to hegemony by
one side, they denounce the division of the world
into military blocs, whose very existence, in
their eyes, creates dangerous tension.[56] Moreover, nonalignment is a comprehensive doctrine
aiming at structural changes in the international system.

*Armed permanent neutrality v. disarmament
under the auspices of nonalignment?*
    As mentioned above, permanent neutrality im-
poses on countries that opt for this status the
obligation to provide for their own defense in
accordance with the international standard. As
long as other states maintain armed forces, permanently neutral states must follow suit. Consequently, a shift to civil, i.e., nonviolent,
defense is out of the question, even if the political conditions in a permanently neutral state
would seem to ideally lend themselves to this
alternative to armed violence. Instead of leading the way in laying down their weapons, the

permanently neutral countries are, on the contrary, the last states allowed to do so.

The nonaligned states are among the most outspoken critics of the arms race.[57] At their very
first summit in Belgrade in 1961, they devoted
six of the twenty-seven points of the Declaration
adopted there to questions of disarmament and
arms control.[58] The desire to slow down and reverse the development and accumulation of military hardware has remained one of their main concerns over the years. Their call for a special
session of the UN General Assembly on disarmament
(or a world disarmament conference) at the 1961
Belgrade conference—last reiterated by the participants in the Colombo summit in 1976—finally met
with a positive response from the other states.
In fact, a Special Session of the UN General Assembly on Disarmament was convened in 1978. Its
concrete results, however, were rather meager,
despite agreement on a fairly lengthy (but not
binding) final document.[59]

The interest of the nonaligned countries in
ending the arms race is obvious. The gap in their
power potential, especially vis-à-vis the countries ahead of them in military technology, would
be gradually bridged. The huge sums spent on ad-
ding new, more sophisticated, and more expensive
weapons to the arsenals of industrialized countries could instead be channeled into the development of the Third World.

Consequently, there seems to exist another fundamental difference between the permanently neutral states—which, whether they like it or not,
are involved in traditional (military) power
politics—and the nonaligned movement, which actively campaigns for a better, more peaceful
world. Yet although they emphasize the necessity of maintaining the balance of forces between the major blocs, the permanently neutral
states too support disarmament initiatives.

They offer their conference facilities to arms-
control negotiators. SALT I took place in Hel-
sinki and Vienna, SALT II in Geneva, the
MURFAAMCE negotiations are being held in Vienna,
and the SALT II agreements were also signed in
the Austrian capital. To mention just another
recent example, Sweden and Austria played a particularly active role during the 1978 Special
Session of the UN General Assembly on Disarmament.[60]

Moreover, in their actual practice, the nonaligned countries do not refrain from acquiring
weapons. At the Lusaka Conference, they declared that international peace and security were
to be safeguarded through the development not
only of the social, economic, and political
strengths of each country but also of the military strength.[61] It is quite understandable that
these countries too try to provide for their security by conventional means, i.e., armed force—
but then, they cannot claim to be different from
other states. Despite the limited economic and
financial resources of the buyer countries, arms
trade with the Third World is continously increasing.[62] What is more, nonaligned states are
also actually using their military hardware,
even against each other, e.g., in the Horn of
Africa, in Indochina, and more recently between
Iraq and Iran, whereas no permanently neutral
state has ever committed an act of aggression.
Once again, reality is thus more complex than
declarations of principle might suggest.

*Permanent neutrality and nonalignment
in the East-West conflict*
In addition to the traditional difficulties of
maintaining independence and neutrality inherent
in a precarious status, permanently neutral states
are faced with new problems brought about by recent developments in international relations.

Permanent neutrality originated in an international system in which war was an acceptable and frequently employed instrument of foreign policy. The law of neutrality therefore focuses on the military (and governmental) sector. Even Austria's permanent neutrality was established between the parties to the cold war at a time when their resorting to armed force could not be ruled out.

The first novel dilemma that confronts permanently neutral states is the growing obsolescence of war in a technical sense.[63] The decisive legal criterion for the existence of the state of war is *animus belligerendi*—i.e., the belligerents' intention to break off all peaceful relations with the enemy and to apply the international law of war instead of the law of peace—and not the outbreak of armed hostilities! If only to avoid the odium of openly violating the prohibition of resorting to war, states nowadays refrain from issuing declarations of war, that would prove their *animus belligerendi* beyond any doubt. They nevertheless pursue their foreign-policy goals by force of arms short of war which they try to justify, more or less plausibly, as (preventive) self-defense, reprisals, humanitarian intervention, etc. Since permanently neutral states have undertaken to observe the law of neutrality in future only in regard to wars as defined under international law, they could refuse to do so in armed conflicts fought without *animus belligerendi*. Yet usually, they do at least abide by the main neutrality obligations for reasons of political prudence.

The situation was further complicated by the trend towards subtler forms of violence. Formerly, regular armed forces of states in uniform used to fight battles on the front with conventional weapons. Nowadays, civil strife,

often by proxy, i.e., supported by other states—
in which the parties rely on the methods of guerrilla strategy—and indirect aggression are increasingly replacing "classical" interstate warfare.

The permanent neutrals are skating on even thin-
ner legal and political ice since the East-West
conflict crucial to their status gave way to détente (or "peaceful coexistence").[64] Both camps
involved now agree that an armed clash must be
avoided, because it may lead to mutual annihilation in the thermonuclear age. The center of
gravity of the nonetheless ongoing confrontation
has therefore shifted to the economic sphere and
to the ideological plane. On the economic level,
East and West not only cooperate, especially in
areas where their interests happen to be com-
plementary, they are simultaneously engaged also
in more than normal competition in which each
side attempts to demonstrate the superiority of
its economic system. Both parties hope that
their examples will prove contagious and will
eventually be followed by the opponent too.

On the ideological front, the "Socialist" bloc
has always insisted that confrontation must not
be renounced. The other side has taken up the
gauntlet. Probably to its own surprise, the
West finds itself on the offensive with its
human rights campaign which encourages similar
claims by dissidents in the socialist camp.

The permanently neutral states cannot (and do
not wish to) sit on the fence in this variant
of the East-West conflict. They never made a
secret of the fact that they are to be counted
among the pluralist democracies with (at least
partly) market-oriented, liberal economies. They
are therefore by no means neutral in these respects, but must be included in the Western camp.

In contrast, the original common denominator

of nonalignment was the desire not to be involved in the cold war. It was in this conflict
that the countries concerned opted for a neutral
position in principle. They saw it as contrary
to their interests to side with either of the
two blocs, whose very existence, in their opinion, posed a continuous threat to world peace
and whose dissolution they therefore advocated.
Furthermore, from the point of view of the developing nonaligned states, both East and West
belong to the opposite camp of industrialized
countries, due to their advanced economic development.

When it comes to actual political behavior,
however, the line of cleavage between nonaligned
and permanently neutral states again turns out
to be less clear-cut than the above statements
of principle suggest.

The nonaligned movement merely refuses to take
sides once and for all in the East-West conflict. Its members insist on judging each issue separately on its merits and supporting the
side whose cause appears the just one in the
dispute at hand. A quantitative analysis of
their voting behavior in the UN General Assembly
reveals that they often are deeply divided over
East-West questions.[65] On the ideological level,
many nonaligned countries—if only to speed up
their economic and social development—opt for a
one-party political system and economic planning; others prefer pluralist democratic structures and market mechanisms. Hence, they cannot help sympathizing with the side in the East-
West conflict that espouses the same political
values and economic principles. Yet as mentioned above, nonaligned countries underline
their active "bridgemanship" and try to mitigate
the East-West conflict by offering their good
offices, mediation, or arbitration to the parties.

Although the European neutrals reject any legal
obligation to observe neutrality in the struggle
between political and economic systems, they
nevertheless have a vested interest in the reduction of tension between East and West. An atmosphere of détente enlarges their freedom of action
in various fields, as both blocs are then more
inclined to tolerate neutral activities even when
the other side benefits from them. In their
"positive" policy of neutrality, the states in
question therefore also try to build bridges between East and West. They offer their conference
facilities to intersystemic negotiations, such as
CSCE, SALT, or the talks on MURFAAMCE, or their
participation in the verification of arms-control
agreements. If called upon, they are also willing
to assume those other functions for which nonaligned states feel particularly qualified. It
remains to be seen whose services the great powers
prefer. On the whole, the nonaligned countries
may have overestimated their potential in the
light of the trend towards bilateralism in superpower relations. The Big Two usually choose to
settle their problems in face-to-face negotiations, without bringing in a third party.

Consequently, despite different points of de-
parture in principle, nonaligned and permanently
neutral states even meet halfway now and then.
Thus, the European neutrals joined forces with
the nonaligned participants to the Conference on
Security and Cooperation in Europe—namely Cyprus,
Malta, and Yugoslavia—to form the so-called N + N
group. Together they worked for compromise solutions to issues over which East and West were divided, such as confidence-building measures or
human rights. They were instrumental in bringing
about agreement on these and other hotly debated
issues in the Final Act of CSCE. The role played
by these honest brokers in the codification of
détente exceeded their actual power potential as

compared with that of the two blocs led by the
superpowers.

Permanently neutral and nonaligned states in the North-South Conflict

Another conflict will most probably dominate
international relations even more during the next
decades: the dispute caused by the Third World's
demands for a new international economic order
based on greater equality and justice. Its
establishment will require fundamental reforms
of the international economic system and more of
a say for developing countries in political matters.

In this global confrontation, the nonaligned
movement is, of course, not neutral, but rather
the spearhead of the developing world. It acts
as the latter's spokesman in the more political
forums, whereas the Group of 77 represents it as
its economic pressure group.

Whether they like it or not, the permanently
neutral states in Europe are entrenched in the opposite camp of the industrialized, rich, developed
countries, to whom the demands of the South are
addressed. The neutrals are sometimes accused of
having sided with the colonial powers during the
first phase of the North-South conflict, the
struggle for legal and political decolonization
of dependent territories in the Third World. It
was on this front that the nonaligned movement
developed, in addition to its negative posture
of noninvolvement in the cold war—a positive common ground. Although it is true enough that the
European neutrals frequently voted with the West
on colonial issues in the UN General Assembly,[66]
this need not necessarily be attributed to a
basically colonialist position; it might also be
explained by certain radical formulations to
which those states refused to subscribe, although they did not object to decolonization in

principle.[67] In recent years, at any rate, they
have unequivocally condemned the remaining ves-
tiges of colonialism in Southern Africa and have
denounced apartheid and racial discrimination.

Moreover, upon closer analysis, nonaligned opposition to colonialism turns out to be impressive in situations of high visibility and low
costs, such as votes in the UN General Assembly;
it is less consistent if relatively little publicity is to be gained and if the disadvantages
involved are considerable. Although the reasons
for such deviations from the agreed upon policy
are understandable, the fact remains that, for
example, neither the rupture of air and sea communications nor the severing of trade links with
South Africa urged by the 1964 Cairo Summit of
the nonaligned group was carried out by all its
members.[68]

The European neutrals can ill afford to steer a
collision course in the current, second phase of
the North-South conflict, in which the emphasis
has shifted to the socioeconomic level. They cannot expect to be treated as neutral bystanders by
either side, especially not by the developing
world. Because of their particular vulnerabili-
ty—due both to the size of their economies and to
their being prohibited from remedying this weakness through economic integration with other
countries—the permanently neutral states have a
special stake in the avoidance of an all-out
North-South confrontation. Hence, they ought to
try to help settle this conflict, together with
other like-minded countries, if possible. They
should conceive methods of implementing the new
international economic order that would be bene-
ficial to both sides and thus would move it beyond the present zero-sum game perspective. For
instance, Western engineers looking for a job
might be employed to develop adequate technolo-
gies for the Third World. "Bridgemanship"

performed by the European neutrals in the North-
South conflict could be facilitated by their own
awareness that their interests do not wholly co-
incide with those of the great economic powers.
Furthermore, they may be acceptable to the South
in this role because of their noncolonial creden-
tials—in point of fact, none of the states in
question ever embarked on overseas colonialism.
If they wish to be credible, however, in the eyes
of the Third World, mere lip service to the noble
cause will not suffice. Those of them that are
lagging behind in this regard will have to increase their development assistance.

Conclusions

From the above analysis, it cannot, of course,
be inferred that there are no far-reaching differences between permanently neutral and nonaligned
states. In terms of numbers, geographical location, economic development and systems, political
structures, legal status, and basic positions in
the two global conflicts of our age, they are indeed fundamentally dissimilar. Equally important
is the fact that the two categories of states per-
ceive each other as different.

Yet there are also quite a few interests that
they have in common. They are relatively power-
less and should therefore strive to reduce tension
between the great powers in order to enhance their
own freedom of action. Although these countries
have at their disposal a number of strategies for
maintaining their independence,[69] it remains to be
seen whether they will succeed in preventing the
erosion of their sovereignty. They are confronted
with a number of similar economic difficulties;
small developed states that are excluded from integration with other countries beyond a low
threshold of intensity are, in fact, facing the
threat of occupying an increasingly peripheral

position within the industrialized world. Hence, they should better understand the problems with which the developing countries are struggling on a global scale. Moreover, when it comes to actual behavior in the international arena, permanently neutral and nonaligned states are not as far apart as they could be expected to be against the background of the above distinctions. It is therefore hardly surprising that the neutrals are by now regularly invited to attend nonaligned summits as guests. The conclusion to be drawn from this paper is that mutually entertained clichés should be corrected. They ought to give way to more balanced views that take complex realities into account.

Notes

1. P. Willetts, *The Non-Aligned Movement: The Origins of a Third World Alliance* (New York: Nichols Publishing Co., 1978). Willetts's quantitative analysis does not go beyond 1970. Although highly desirable, further empirical research along the same lines in order to bring his findings up to date would exceed the scope of this article. For a recent step in this direction see Klaus Burri, *The Non-Aligned Developing Countries, 1968-1972: Voting Agreement in the UN General Assembly and Foreign Relations with the Soviet Union and the USA,* Kleine Studien zur politischen Wissenschaft no. 176 (Zurich: Forschungsstelle für politische Wissenschaft, Universität Zürich, 1979). After completing the present article, I received a paper on the topic under discussion written by D. Frei, *Neutrality and Non-Alignment, Convergencies and Contrasts,* Kleine Studien zur politischen Wissenschaft no. 175 (Zurich: Forschungsstelle für politische Wissenschaft, Universität Zürich, 1979), but it was too late to include Frei's points and conclusions here.

2. Most of the literature on this topic is German, the dominant language in Switzerland and Austria, which are the only two genuine permanently neutral states. Since this paper is addressed mainly to English-speaking readers, only some major scholarly works in German will be quoted. For a recent summary, see A. Verdross, *The Permanent Neutrality of Austria* (Vienna: Verlag für Geschichte und Politik, 1978), and the literature quoted therein.

3. The Fifth and Thirteenth Hague Conventions of 1907 deserve particular mention in this context. Changes in the nonlegal context since 1907 have, of course, affected the applicability of some of those "classical" norms.

4. Hence, they cannot be circumvented by observing the principle of impartiality (see category 3), one of the "pillars" of neutrality; even if the neutral state (the traditional prohibition does not apply to individual citizens) were to grant all belligerents exactly the same amount of military aid, such support would still constitute a breach of the law of neutrality. The legal situation would be different if all warring parties agreed to deviations from this principle.

5. It stands to reason that the material consequences of such formally equal treatment—which suffices under international law—may differ considerably. In the illustration given in the text, this would be the case, for example, if only one side has previously imported the embargoed product from the neutral state, whereas the other grew it on its own territory. Formal impartiality will, in such a constellation, favor the latter and hurt the former. The neutrals will be well advised, if the crucial credibility of their status is to be maintained, to see to it that the adverse net effects of at least several such restrictive measures also are as balanced as possible.

For this reason, Switzerland introduced the yardstick of the *courant normal* during World War II:
It tried to maintain commercial relations with
the belligerents along prewar lines. The Swiss
government always insisted, however, on the op-
tional character of this decision.

6. *Schweizerisches Jahrbuch für internationales Recht* (1957), pp. 195 ff.

7. K. Zemanek, "Gutachten zu den von dem Volks-
begehren zur Abschaffung des Bundesheeres (Bundes-
heervolksbegehren) aufgeworfenen neutralitäts-
rechtlichen und neutralitätspolitischen Fragen,"
Österreichische Zeitschrift für Aussenpolitik
(Vienna) 10 (1970):128 ff.

8. The relevant statistics are contained in
the *Military Balance,* published each year by the
International Institute for Strategic Studies,
London.

9.   A. Verdross, "Austria's Permanent Neutrality and the United Nations Organization," *American
Journal of International Law* 50 (1956):61 ff.;
K. Zemanek, "Neutral Austria in the United Nations," *International Organization* 15 (1961):
408 ff.; H. F. Koeck, "A Permanently Neutral State
in the Security Council," *Cornell International
Law Journal* 6 (1973):137 ff.

10. Furthermore, these considerations are—alas!—
highly academic anyway, as disagreement among the
permanent members of the Security Council has up
to now led time and again to the use of their
"veto power," with the result that the UN system
of collective security has, in practice, remained
a dead letter.

11. K. Zemanek, "Zeitgemässe Neutralität?"
Österreichische Zeitschrift für Aussenpolitik 16
(1976):358.

12. Which is by no means restricted to the permanently neutral state's foreign affairs, but en-
compasses all sectors of its political activity.

13. The reasons why they are in a better position to make such classical contributions to the
mitigation of international conflicts and the im-
provement of international cooperation are fairly
obvious. With respect to good offices, mediation,
and peacekeeping, the states involved in the conflict must believe in the impartiality of the
third party willing to engage in these functions;
as regards headquarters of international organizations and venues of international conferences,
each member or participant should feel that he
is sending his delegates to a friendly state's
territory.

14. The permanently neutral states that by
definition are small powers are thus aware that
they cannot really hope to resist a large-scale
attack launched by a great power or by a group
of allied states against them. What they are
confident to be able to achieve is rather to influence the potential aggressors' cost-benefit
calculations in their favor. They are therefore
well advised to exceed the threshold of the international minimum standard—which they are legally bound to reach—in their defensive efforts.
E. Spannocchi, "Verteidigung ohne Selbstzerstö-
rung," in E. Spannocchi and G. Brossolet, *Verteidigung ohne Schlacht* (Munich and Vienna:
Carl Hanser Verlag, 1976), pp. 15 ff.

15. From a historic perspective, Belgium and
Luxembourg (from 1831-39 and 1867, respectively
until the First World War) have to be added to
the list of permanently neutral states.

16. G. Maude, *The Finnish Dilemma: Neutrality in the Shadow of Power* (London, New York,
Toronto: Oxford University Press, 1976);

D. Woker, *Die skandinavischen Neutralen* (Berne and Stuttgart: Verlag Paul Haupt, 1978).

17. H. Neuhold, "La neutralité du Laos," *Österreichische Zeitschrift für öffentliches Recht* 19 (1969):187 ff.

18. Whether Ireland is to be included among the permanently neutral states is open to question; true enough, it has not joined any military alliance, but it did become a member of the European Communities—a step contrary to permanently neutral status. See P. Keatinge, *The Formulation of Irish Foreign Policy* (Dublin: Institute of Public Administration, 1973), pp. 24 ff.

19. Surprisingly few comprehensive works have been written on nonalignment. Notable exceptions include: L. W. Martin, ed., *Neutralism and Non-Alignment: The New States in World Affairs* (New York: Frederick A. Praeger, 1962); B. Sen, *Against the Cold War* (Bombay: Asia Publishing House, 1962); P. Lyon, *Neutralism* (Leicester: Leicester University Press, 1963); P. F. Power, *Neutralism and Disengagement* (New York: Scribner Research Anthologies, 1964); C. V. Crabb, *The Elephants and the Grass: A Study of Non-Alignment* (New York: Frederick A. Praeger, 1965); Y. Etinger and O. Metikyan, *The Policy of Non-Alignment* (Moscow: Progress Publishers, 1966); G. H. Jansen, *Afro-Asia and Non-Alignment* (London: Faber and Faber, 1955); J. W. Burton, ed., *Non-Alignment* (London: Andre Deutsch, 1966); J. W. Burton, *International Relations: A General Theory* (London: Cambridge University Press, 1967), pp. 163 ff.; L. Acimovic, ed., *Non-Alignment in the World of Today* (Belgrade: Institute of International Politics and Economics, 1959); L. Mates, *Non-Alignment: Theory and Current Policy* (Dobbs Ferry, N.Y.: Oceana Publications, 1972); and Willetts, *The Non-Aligned Movement*. A comprehensive collection of documents

on nonalignment was compiled by O. Jankowitsch and K. P. Sauvant in *The Third World Without Superpowers: The Collected Documents of the Non-Aligned Countries* (Dobbs Ferry, N.Y.: Oceana Publications, 1978).

20.   Even Yugoslavia, one of the protagonists of the movement, developed as a result of a process of trial and error.   As late as 1954, it, in fact, agreed to transform the 1933 Balkan Treaty with Greece and Turkey into a formal military alliance.   Willetts, p. 4, n. 1.

21.   This qualification was already contained in the "Five Commandments of Nonalignment" agreed upon at the 1961 preparatory meeting in Cairo that set the stage for the first Summit in Belgrade.

22.   *United Nations Treaty Series* 299:90 ff.

23.   Q. L. Focsaneanu, "Les 'cinq principes' de coexistence et le droit international," *Annuaire français de droit international* 2 (1965):150 ff.

24.   Dulles condemned neutrality as an "immoral and shortsighted conception." Lyon, *Neutralism*, p. 67, n. 19.

25.   The Afro-Asian Conference held in the Indonesian city of Bandung in 1955 should not be included among the nonaligned meetings because it was also attended by Western and Communist allies such as Japan, the Philippines, Turkey, and South Vietnam on the one hand and North Vietnam and the People's Republic of China on the other.   B. Jevtić, "Die internationale Rolle der Blockfreiheit," I, *Internationale Politik*, no. 640 (1976), p. 7; Willetts, *The Non-Aligned Movement*, p. 3, n. 1.

26.   Jankowitsch and Sauvant, *The Third World*, pp. 3, 19, 44 ff.   In addition, it was more

than a coincidence that the nonaligned movement
was carried by strong and colorful personalities,
such as Presidents Nasser, Nehru, Nkrumah, Sukarno, and Tito during its first phase. See K. W.
Deutsch, *The Analysis of International Relations*
(Englewood Cliffs, N.J.:   Prentice-Hall, 1968),
pp. 198 ff.

27. R. Emerson, "Self-Determination," *American Journal of International Law* 65 (1971):459 ff.

28. The Nigerian civil war and the armed hostilities in the Horn of Africa may only have been
forerunners.

29. Burton, *International Relations,* p. 163 f.,
n. 19, p. 232 ff.

30. OAS is therefore not included among the
military alliances "concluded in the context of
Great Power conflicts." Moreover, the nonaligned
states perhaps hope that admission to their ranks
will facilitate the withdrawal of OAS members
from this regional organization dominated by a
super power or will at least encourage a more independent policy. O. Jankowitsch and K. P. Sauvant, "The Evolution of the Non-Aligned Movement
into a Pressure Group for the Establishment of
the New International Economic Order," (Paper de-
livered at the seventeenth Annual Convention of
the International Studies Association, Toronto,
1976), p. 13.

31. See the Declaration and the Programme of
Action on the Establishment of a New International
Economic Order adopted by the UN General Assembly
at its Sixth Special Session in 1974 in Resolutions 3201 (S-VI) and 3202 (S-VI).

32. On the other hand, the common economic
position did not spill over into the political
sector. Political conflicts and even armed
hostilities continue to break out between

nonaligned states and do weaken the movement.
At the time of writing, controversies over the
suspension of Egypt, one of the founding members,
because of its peace treaty with Israel and the
representation of Kampuchea after the overthrow
of the Pol Pot regime looming large on the political horizon.

33. Jankowitsch and Sauvant, "The Evaluation
of the Non-Aligned Movement," pp. 13 ff., n. 30;
O. Jankowitsch, "Neue Modelle zwischenstaatlicher
Zusammenarbeit: Organisation und Institutionen
der Blockfreien," *Österreichische Zeitschrift für
Aussenpolitik* 17 (1977):214 ff; Willetts, *The
Non-Aligned Movement*, pp. 36 ff., n. 1.

34. The nonaligned states also established a
few funds. Willetts, *The Non-Aligned Movement*,
p. 43, n. 1.

35. This was already specified at the preparatory meeting held in Cairo in 1961, which paved
the way for the Belgrade summit. Jankowitsch and
Sauvant, *The Third World*, pp. XXXI f., n. 19.

36. Willetts, *The Non-Aligned Movement*, pp.
127-28, n. 1. Nine of the twenty-five "radical
core group" states that attended the 1961 Belgrade summit had strong military ties with the
United States or the United Kingdom (ibid., p. 23).

37. See R. Petković, "Die Entwicklung der Dok-
trin und Bewegung der Blockfreiheit," *Internationale Politik* 27, no. 636 (1976), p. 13.

38. Their joint action within the framework
of the Conference on Security and Cooperation
in Europe should be singled out in this respect.
Frei, *Neutrality and Non-Alignment*, pp. 6-7, n. 1.

39. Burton, *International Relations*, pp. 195 ff.,
n. 19. One of the gravest errors committed by
Western governments was to equate economic planning and the prohibition of opposition parties

in the Third World (both of which were dictated by the desire to accelerate development) with communism. They overlooked the strong nationalism of young states that prevented them from throwing in their lot with the "Socialist" bloc.

40. D. Vital, *The Inequality of States: A Study of the Small Power in International Relations* (Oxford: At the Clarendon Press, 1967), pp. 39 ff.

41. I have developed this point at length elsewhere. See H. Neuhold, "Der Wandel im System der internationalen Beziehungen," *Österreichische Zeitschrift für Aussenpolitik* 15 (1975): 344 ff.

42. H. Maull, *Oil and Influence: The Oil Weapon Examined*, Adelphi Paper no. 117 (London, 1975); E. N. Krapels, *Oil and Security: Problems and Prospects of Importing Countries*, Adelphi Paper no. 136 (London, 1977).

43. A general theory of neutral policy in a broad, political-science sense was developed by D. Frei, *Dimensionen neutraler Politik*, Etudes et Travaux; de l'Institut Universitaire des Hautes Etudes Internationales no. 8 (Geneva, 1969).

44. It separates NATO forces in the North and in Central Europe from the Southern Tier.

45. Denmark and Norway do not permit the presence of foreign armed forces or nuclear weapons on their territories in time of peace.

46. A. Wolfers, *Discord and Collaboration: Essays on International Politics* (Baltimore: Johns Hopkins University Press, 1965), pp. 73 ff.

47. Defined by the International Court of Justice in the North Sea Continental Shelf Cases as follows: "The States concerned must therefore feel that they are conforming to what

amounts to a legal obligation." *I.C.J. Report*, 1969, p. 44.

48. Burton, *International Relations*, p. 221, n. 19; Willetts, *The Non-Aligned Movement*, p. 20, n. 1.

49. Lyon, *Neutralism*, p. 64, n. 19.

50. Neuhold, "Neutralité du Laos," (Der Wandel im System), pp. 327 ff., n. 41, and the literature quoted here.

51. Verdross, "Austria's Permanent Neutrality," p. 13, n. 2.

52. D. Frei, "Kleinstaatliche Aussenpolitik als Umgang mit Abhängigkeit," in *Die Schweiz in einer sich wandelnden Welt*, D. Frei, ed. (Zurich: Schulthess Polygraphischer Verlag, 1977), p. 222.

53. Frei, *Neutralität—Ideal oder Kalkül?* (Frauenfeld and Stuttgart: Verlag Hüber, 1967).

54. Lyon, *Neutralism*, pp. 67 ff., n. 19; Willetts, *The Non-Aligned Movement*, pp. 5 ff, n. 1.

55. Ibid., p. 21, n. 1.

56. Jevtić, "Die internationale Rolle," p. 7, n. 25.

57. B. Jevtić, "Die internationale Rolle der Blockfreiheit," part II, *Internationale Politik*, no. 641 (1976), pp. 13 ff.; Willetts, *The Non-Aligned Movement*, pp. 23 ff., n. 1.

58. Jankowitsch and Sauvant, *The Third World*, pp. 3 ff., n. 19.

59. UN Document A/RES/S-10/2; text in 17 *International Legal Materials* (1978), pp. 1016 ff.

60. E. Suchapipa, "Die Sondergeneralversammlung der Vereinten Nationen über Abrüstung (23. Mai-30. Juni 1978)," *Österreichische Zeitschrift für Aussenpolitik* 18 (1978):112 ff.

61.   Jankowitsch and Sauvant, *The Third World*, p. 83, n. 19.

62.   See the relevant figures in the Yearbooks of the Stockholm International Peace Research Institute.

63.   Only the Arab-Israeli conflict was undoubtedly fought as a war in the legal sense. D. Schindler, "Der Kriegszustand im Völkerrecht der Gegenwart," in *Um Recht und Freiheit: Festschrift für August Freiherr von der Heydte*, ed. H. Kipp, F. Mayer, A. Steinkamm (Berlin: Duncker & Humbolt, 1977), pp. 555 ff.

64.   H. Neuhold, "Military, Economic and Ideological Ambiguities of Détente: Theory and Reality," 32 (1979):153.

65.   Willetts, *The Non-Aligned Movement*, pp. 137 ff., n. 1.

66.   Ibid., p. 19, n. 1, pp. 159 ff.

67.   Austria abstained, for instance, when resolution 32/296 on Namibia was voted upon in the UN General Assembly. The resolution called upon member states to render not only material and financial assistance but also military aid to the South West Africa People's Organization to enable it to intensify its struggle for the liberation of Namibia. It might be necessary to equate this with support for colonialism if a cluster analysis of the votes cast in the General Assembly is undertaken; such a simplification does not correspond, however, to the much more complex political reality.

68.   Willetts, *The Non-Aligned Movement*, pp. 167 ff., n. 1.

69.   D. Frei, *Kleinstaatliche Aussenpolitik*, pp. 201 ff., n. 52.

CHARLES W. YOST

Concluding Observations

As the final speaker—I would like to express my great appreciation—on my behalf and, I am sure, on behalf of all the other participants—to our hosts, the Austrian Consulate General and the Austrian Institute, for arranging this excellent symposium and for their hospitality. It has certainly been most enlightening to me, and I think all those who participated have not only enjoyed it but have profited by it, and we are most grateful.

I am going to be very brief—first, because it is late in the day and you all have been very patient, and second, because my association with Austria (though I was assigned there twice) was a long time ago. So I am going to limit myself to two things: one, a few brief impressions and recollections of my assignment there during the period we have been discussing, and second, a few comments on some of the remarks that have been made by other speakers on various aspects of developments during that period.

First, the impressions: I think it's so important to emphasize (as other speakers have emphasized) the intangible side of the Austrian miracle. It was due in substantial part—as others have suggested—to one of the most extraordinary displays of national leadership that I have encountered anywhere in my diplomatic career. I can't imagine where this body of men—Renner, Figl, Schärf, Raab, Gruber, Helmer, Körner—could have been matched during this postwar period anywhere else in the world. They

were courageous, they were ingenious, they were
adroit; they knew when to be flexible and when
to be firm. It was a great privilege for me to
have known them all very well.

I can remember during my first assignment in
1947-49 that Julius Raab was not permitted by
the Soviets to participate in the government
because of alleged anti-Soviet views. But I
used to see a great deal of him, and he was of
course tremendously influential in running the
People's Party, even at that time. Those were
times of great hardship, and I can remember going often to *Heurigen* with him, when he supplied
the wine and we supplied the food. Since we had
a cook who had been for many years with Sacher's,
I think Mr. Raab enjoyed those occasions.

But it was not only the leadership, of course,
it was the Austrian people themselves who displayed amazing resolution and determination—particularly those in the Soviet zone, who for a
period of ten years lived under the constant
threat of Soviet pressure (and sometimes the
threats were carried out) and in a much more
poverty-stricken and deprived state than those
in the Western zone. They withstood this marvelously.

And the people of Vienna—I was always amazed
at the rapidity and zest with which they revived
their cultural life. The opera, despite the
destruction of the building, immediately resumed
in the Theater an der Wien with marvelous artists like Schoeffler, Kunz, Schwarzkopf, Jurinac;
the concerts, the orchestras, were revived with
some of the greatest musicians in the world.
The carnival season was celebrated with the most
intense enthusiasm and indefatigability. While
in a way these things may seem frivolous, they
were far from being so, because they represented
the heart of Viennese life that was so promptly
and marvelously restored. I don't think I have

ever experienced over a period of a couple of years such cultural abundance as one encountered there.

Now to move from that and say a few words about the Allied Council and the presence of Allied forces and their participation in the council. The Western Allies did, of course, provide substantial and indispensible support to the Austrian government and people; with all their courage, they could not have managed had the Soviets been there alone, and not the Westerners. You only have to look at Czechoslovakia next door (where I had spent about a year before I moved down to Austria) to make a comparison—despite the fact that they also had some very courageous leaders. Though Benesch and Masaryk were pretty well burnt out, there were others who were courageous, but nevertheless they were unable to resist. It was, in a way, an anomaly that the Western powers, having assumed the responsibility for the occupation of Austria, took a very active part in preserving Austrian independence and liberties; and since the Western powers had no occupation responsibilities for Czechoslovakia (a neighboring liberated country) and since, as the cold war intensified, we were encountering responsibilities all over the world—in Greece, in Turkey, in the Mediterranean—we stood aside when Czechoslovakia was overcome.

But we did have some very nervous moments in Austria that I can remember. Particularly during the Berlin blockade there was great apprehension in many quarters that this action would be repeated in Vienna. I can well remember one night when two Soviet pilots defected with one of their most modern planes, landing in the American zone of Austria. Of course the Russians demanded their instant return to the Soviet Union, and as I say, there were people on our side who feared that if we did not comply, they might clamp down a blockade. All that night we conferred by teletype with Washington. As dawn broke, we triumphed and told the Russians: "Sorry, we are keeping these people. You can have the plane back after we have stripped it of all its interesting equipment."

Also, the Allied Council went through a routine procedure that was less sensational, but probably just as important in defending Austrian rights. I myself certainly learned a great deal about negotiating with the Soviets during those long sessions, which I think were ultimately constructive. The role of the Marshall Plan has just been referred to. That should not be forgotten, not only for its financial contribution but because the Western countries' being ready and willing to pour those substantial sums into the country was a political indication of the importance we attached to it. Hence it served as a morale builder as well as providing essential supplies.

So much for recollections. Just a few words about some of the points that have been made. It is a most interesting historical perception that neither the United States nor the Soviet Union were properly prepared for the occupation of Austria or had a clear plan as to what they were going to do. The stalemate or the failure to accomplish much for a long time in the European Advisory Commission was indeed—as has been noted—a reflection of President Roosevelt's reluctance to get into political planning for the postwar period. This reluctance had some very sensible bases. We know that many of these postwar problems were extremely controversial and might have weakened Allied unity if settlements were attempted while the war was still going on. Also, Roosevelt argued that one should not prejudge the decisions of the peoples of Europe

after they had been liberated by trying to impose
on them settlements devised in Washington or London or Moscow. Both of those reasons were true
enough, but nevertheless, in my opinion, much
more planning should have been done. After all,
you fight a war not merely to defeat the enemy,
but to create certain political situations. We
should have given more attention to this objective. There was a great deal of postwar planning
going on in the State Department under Mr. Hull
and Leo Pesvalsky, but it was not really reflected
in the White House or in high-level policy. And
the Soviets as well had not really made up their
minds.

It has been my theory for some time that immediately after the war Stalin had only decided
that he must control the situation in Poland and
Rumania (and possibly in Bulgaria) and must have
substantial, if not predominant, influence in
Germany. But at the outset he had probably not
felt that it would be necessary to control countries immediately to the West of those. That,
I think, is borne out by the fact that free elections were permitted in the first few months
after the war, not only in Austria but in Czechoslovakia and Hungary. It was only as the cold
war intensified that he presumably reached the
conclusion that he must more effectively control
these other countries as well. He was prevented
from doing this in Austria for reasons we have
been talking about, but he clamped down at once
in Hungary and Czechoslovakia. Also, in Austria
it was not only the Western presence that determined the outcome but the fact that Stalin's
initial policy gave a good deal of leeway to the
people of Austria, allowing them to vote freely
and providing a chance for this remarkable body
of leaders to establish themselves, to set up a
going concern, and to foil any subsequent attempts to undermine the liberties of the country.

Now finally, a few words about the treaty and the balance advantage from it. I have always thought there were two important elements in bringing about the treaty in 1955. One was Khrushchev's personal desire to participate in a summit with Eisenhower and the other leaders as the symbol of the restoration of the Soviet Union to full equality. I think one must never forget the personal aspects involved in decisions of this kind. Another element might have been what we were talking about a few minutes ago: the military developments in Austria, which were relatively insignificant in size, but which nevertheless may have given the Soviets the feeling that, if they waited too long, Austria might be more and more integrated into the Western military system. That was a danger that could be avoided by a treaty and neutralization.

People often ask what the lessons of the Austrian peace treaty are. I am afraid that there aren't any that could be applied to the present situation. The factors there were unique and are certainly not likely to be repeated now, as we see in Poland at the moment. It may be that there was even an advantage to Austria from the four-power occupation, not only in keeping out the Soviets or holding them at bay but also in creating an Austrian national identity—a unity in opposition to all of the occupying powers— and in producing the coalition between the two great parties, which had been at swords' points and had fought each other in the prewar period. Due to wise leadership the two coalition parties maintained this coalition throughout the occupation because they saw that it served them well and was indeed necessary.

But I would think that certainly the West gained from the treaty and the final liberation of Austria far more than the Soviets. Here we have, in the center of Europe, a brilliant

example of the advantages of freedom, free enterprise, and association with the West—a standing
reproach to the dictatorships further east, which
are unable to provide anywhere nearly so well for
their peoples. I think when tourists from the
East, including Soviets, walk down the Kärntner-
strasse or the Kohlmarkt, that must be one of the
most subversive influences they could be subjected to. This, I think, is again an intangible, but it makes an important contribution to
the stability of central Europe at the present
time and perhaps to the evolving extension of
freedom further east, which we trust will be
peaceful.

Contributors

Contributors

Ware Adams, U.S. Diplomat (ret.). Director of the U.S. Political Division of the Allied Commission for Austria, 1945-47. Member of the U.S. delegation to the London meeting on the Austrian State Treaty of the deputy foreign ministers, 1947. Author: "A Memoir of Austria," published in *Tales of the Foreign Service* (Columbia: University of South Carolina Press, 1978).

William B. Bader, Vice-President, SRI-International, Washington. Former Chief of Staff, Committee on Foreign Relations, United States Senate. Author: *Austria between East and West, 1945-1955* (Stanford, Calif.: Stanford University Press, 1966).

Robert A. Bauer, Representative of the Organization for International Economic Relations, Vienna, in the United States and at the Economic and Social Council of the United Nations. Consultant, Brookings Institution and Johns Hopkins Foreign Policy Institute. Former U.S. Diplomat and Professor of Political Science. Director, Austrian Freedom Broadcasting Station, Fécamp, France, 1939-40. Voice of America commentator to Austria 1942-48. Editor: *The United States in World Affairs: Leadership, Partnership, or Disengagement?* and *The Interaction of Economics and Foreign Policy* (Charlottesville: University Press of Virginia, 1975).

Fritz Bock, President, Creditanstalt-Bankverein and of the Organization for International Economic Relations, Vienna; former Austrian Vice-Chancellor and Minister of Trade and Reconstruction. Author: *Der Anschluss an Europa* (Vienna: Verlag Niederösterreichisches Pressehaus, 1978).

Halvor O. Ekern, U.S. Diplomat (ret.). Military officer, 1945. U.S. Director of the Quadripartite Secretariat of the Allied Commission for Austria. Member of the U.S. Delegation to the Austrian State Treaty negotiations, 1947-55.

Martin F. Herz, U.S. Ambassador (ret.). Director of Studies, Institute for the Study of Diplomacy, School of Foreign Service, Georgetown University. With headquarters of United States forces in Austria, 1945. With American Legation, Vienna, 1946-48. Austrian Public Affairs, State Department, 1949-50. Author: *Beginnings of the Cold War* (Bloomington: University of Indiana Press, 1966).

Hanspeter Neuhold, Professor of International Relations and International Law at the University of Vienna and at the Austrian Diplomatic Academy; Director of the Research Institute of the Austrian Association for Foreign Affairs. Author: *International Conflicts—Legal and Illegal Methods of Their Settlement* (Vienna and New York: Springer, 1977).

Robert G. Neumann, Senior Associate, Georgetown University Center for Strategic and International Studies. Former American Ambassador to Afghanistan, Morocco, and Saudi Arabia. Former professor of political science, University of California, Los Angeles.

Manfried Rauchensteiner, Teacher of Austrian
history at the University of Vienna.   Research
fellow at the Museum of Military History, Vienna.   Author: *Der Sonderfall: Die Besatzungszeit in Österreich, 1945-1955* (Graz, Vienna,
Cologne: Styria, 1979).

William L. Stearman, Senior Staff Member, National
Security Council Staff, White House.   Director,
Russian Area Studies Program, Loyola Graduate
School, Georgetown University.   U.S. Representative in the Political Directorate, Subcommittee
of the Allied Commission, Vienna, 1950-55.
Author: *The Soviet Union and the Occupation of
Austria* (Vienna, Bonn, Zurich: Siegler & Co.,
1961).

Adolf Sturmthal, Professor, Institute of Labor
and Industrial Relations, University of Illinois at Urbana-Champaign.   Former assistant to
Friedrich Adler (Secretary-General of the Labour
Socialist Internationale).   Author: *The Tragedy
of European Labour, 1918-1939* (New York: Columbia University Press, 1961).

Charles W. Yost (1907-81), U.S. Ambassador (ret.).
Counselor, American Legation, Vienna, 1947-49.
Deputy High Commissioner to Austria, 1953-54.
Last publication: *History and Memory* (New
York: Norton, 1980).